ISBN 978-1-9998027-4-5

Halima Publishing
Wallingford, Oxfordshire U.K.
www.halimapublishing.co.uk

By Yasmin Watson
Original illustrations by Hana Horack-Elyafi

BOOK TWO

ISLAMIC HISTORY

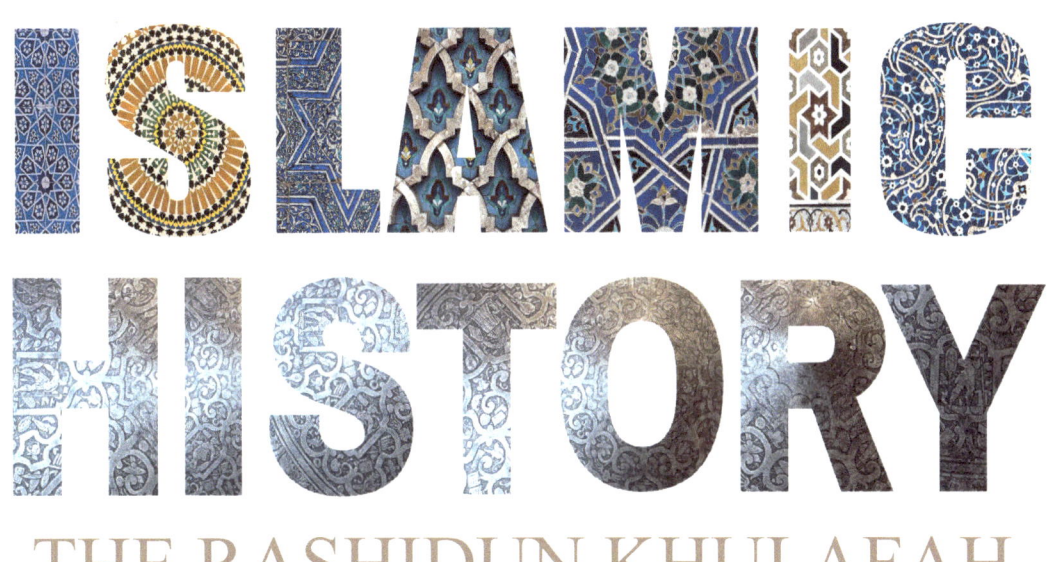

THE RASHIDUN KHULAFAH

THE RIGHTLY GUIDED CALIPHS

ABU BAKR   'UMAR   'UTHMAN   'ALI

Contents

Abu Bakr As-Siddique رض

The Prophet Muhammad ﷺ said these things about Abu Bakr as-Siddique*:

"Never has the sun risen or set on a person, other than a prophet, greater than Abu Bakr."

"What Allah poured into my heart, I poured into the heart of Abu Bakr as Siddique."

"Abu Bakr does not surpass you because of fasting or praying more, but because of a secret that took root in his heart."

"If I were to take an intimate friend (khalil) other than my Lord, I would have chosen Abu Bakr."

"I called people to Islam, everybody thought over it, at least for a while, but this was not the case with Abu Bakr, the moment I put Islam before him, he accepted it without any hesitation."

"Allah will show His glory to the people in a general way, but He will show it to Abu Bakr in a special way."

Others said about him: "It was if he was goodness itself."

Abu Bakr* was referred to in the Qur'an;

"When the unbelievers drove him out, he had no more than one companion. The two were in the Cave, and he said to his companion, Fear not, for Allah is with us." (At-Tawbah: 40)

And (away from the Fire) shall be kept the most faithful who gives his wealth, thereby purifying himself, and seeks to gain no pleasure or reward other than the Presence of his Lord, the Most High. (Al-Layl:17-21)

When Prophet Muhammad ﷺ Left This World

When the Prophet ﷺ died, the Muslims fell into disarray. People were in shock, not believing he had really gone. 'Umar went around saying, "I will strike the head of any man who would say that Muhammad died!" But amidst the chaos, it was Abu Bakr who remained calm and said,

"O People! If anyone among you worshipped Muhammad, let him know that Muhammad is dead. But those who worship Allah, let them know that He lives and will never die. Let all of us recall the words of the Qur'an: 'Muhammad is only a Messenger of Allah, there have been Messengers before him. What then, will you turn back from Islam if he dies or is killed?'" (Aali 'Imraan 3:144)

He reminded the people that it is Allah Whom we worship and that although Muhammad ﷺ was the Prophet of Allah, he was born into a body that lived and died like everyone else, and that in reality, the souls of the prophets are ever-living. Even though Abu Bakr loved the Prophet ﷺ intensely, he was not overcome with grief and bravely was able to counsel the other Companions, remaining steadfast like a rock for the Believers.

WHO SHOULD BE THE KHALIFAH OF ISLAM?

After the Prophet ﷺ left this world, many people assumed things would go back to how they were before the dawn of Islam: they would continue to practise Islam but under the same tribal leaders. Abu Bakr and 'Umar knew that this was not what the Prophet ﷺ wanted, because it would lead to a renewal of the tribal feuds of pre-Islam. A new leader or khalifah needed to be chosen to keep unity among the Muslims, so the Companions immediately met to discuss the new leader.

The two main groups amongst Muslims were the Muhajirun (the immigrants from Makkah), and the Ansar (the people of Medina who welcomed the Muhajirun). The Ansar gathered at their official meeting place. Sa'ad ibn 'Abadah, the Ansar leader, suggested that the khalifah should be from amongst them. The Muhajirun argued that they had a better claim for the khalifah. When the news reached Abu Bakr, he hurried to their gathering, fearing that confusion might spread once again. He said, "Both Muhajirun and Ansar have done great service to Islam. But the former were the first to accept Islam, they were always very close to the Messenger of Allah. So, O Ansar, let the khalifah be from amongst them." After a short discussion, the Ansar agreed that they should choose the khalifah from amongst the Muhajirun, being from the tribe of Quraysh and the first to accept Islam.

ABU BAKR - THE PERFECT CHOICE

They considered how the Holy Prophet ﷺ had already hinted at his choice by only asking Abu Bakr to lead the prayers on numerous occasions and instructing people to go to Bakr when he was no longer available. They also knew many things the Holy Prophet ﷺ had said about the superiority of Abu Bakr, in terms of his faith and his high level of character.

They may have remembered when the tribe of Banu al-Mustaliq requested Anas to ask the Prophet ﷺ, "'If we come next year and do not find you, to whom should we give our charity payment?' The Prophet replied, 'Give them to Abu Bakr!' I told them his answer but they said, 'What if we do not find Abu Bakr?' I conveyed to him the question and he replied, 'Give them to 'Umar!' They asked again. 'What if we do not find Umar?' He said, 'Tell them, give them to Uthman - and may you perish the day 'Uthman is killed!'" These replies by the Prophet ﷺ not only predict the sucession of the khulafah but warn of the day of 'Uthman's death twenty-four years later.

They may also have also remembered that the Prophet ﷺ said, "Take for your leaders the two who come after me, Abu Bakr and 'Umar." (Tirmidhi)

In addition, the Prophet ﷺ ordered the sealing up of all the doors to the Mosque except that of Abu Bakr.

'Umar then put his hand in Abu Bakr's, which was the pledge of allegiance or bayat. Everyone else in that meeting unanimously followed suit. Henceforth, Abu Bakr was proclaimed the next khalifa of Islam.

Arabs discussing inside by Hana Horack-Elyafi

Abu Bakr then addressed the *Jumaat*, the Muslim congregation:

"Help me if I am in the right. Set me right, if I am in the wrong. The weak among you shall be strong with me until, God willing, his rights have been vindicated. The strong among you shall be weak with me until, if God wills, I have taken what is due from him. Obey me as long as I obey Allah and His

'ALI IBN ABI TALIB'S DELAY

Some say that Sayyidina 'Ali did not agree with Abu Bakr being the new khalifah. At the time of the meeting to decide the new khalifah, 'Ali was inside the house of the Prophet ﷺ with a few others and so did not attend. Some narrations say that at first, he even declined to give *bayat* (allegiance) which could have been because of a dissagreement between Abu Bakr and his wife, Fatima, the daughter of the Prophet ﷺ, about some inheritance that Fatima wanted to claim.

Fatima died six months later and 'Ali took *bayat* and explained that he and the others delayed because they may have had more right to the khalifah because of kinship, but that they now recognised Abu Bakr.

'Ali did not hold animosity towards Sayyidina Abu Bakr as-Siddique. We hear from the scholar, Hakim, who narrated that when 'Ali was asked about Abu Bakr he said, "He is a person whom Allah called as-Siddique on the tongue of the Prophet ﷺ and he is the khalifah of the Prophet ﷺ. We accept him for our religion and for our worldly life."

Who was Abu Bakr ?

Abu Bakr as-Siddique, whose full name was 'Abdullah ibn 'Uthman ibn al-Amir ibn 'Amr al-Qurayshi, was born two and half years after the Prophet Muhammad ﷺ in 573. His name means 'Father of the camel' because he used to like looking after camels.

He was the son of 'Uthman and Umm al-Khair who were part of a noble tribe that liked to avoid battle and conflict. Abu Bakr had an incredible understanding of the lineage of the Arabs, he also had a love of poetry and was very articulate.

Abu Bakr was a wealthy businessman when the Prophet Muhammad ﷺ began to receive revelations. His success stemmed from the fact that people liked to do business with him as he was trustworthy and would never cheat, unlike many merchants at that time. He never drank alcohol nor worshipped idols before Islam. He was the best friend of the Prophet ﷺ and his closest Companion.

THE TRUTHFUL ONE

Abu Bakr was called 'Siddique' or 'Truthful', as he always accepted everything the Prophet ﷺ said unquestioningly and without a moment's hesitation. When he heard that the Prophet ﷺ had gone on the miraculous Night Journey to Jerusalem and through all the Heavenly realms to speak directly with Allah, Abu Bakr unhesitatingly accepted it as truth.

In his heart, he had pure certainty of Allah's Word. Abu Bakr was the 'mirror' of the Prophet ﷺ; he always followed him in every deed and action and would never prefer his own desires. He followed his orders to the letter.

UNSURPASSED GENEROSITY

He was also first in material support. While others of the Muslims gave large fortunes in support of their faith, Abu Bakr was the first to give everything he had. When asked what he had left for his children he answered, "Allah and His Prophet." On hearing this 'Umar said, "None can surpass Abu Bakr in serving the cause of Islam."

As a special gift from Allah ﷻ, all of Abu Bakr's family became Muslim at some point which was unusual, even some of the Prophet's ﷺ relatives did not become Muslim.

KINDNESS, COMPASSION AND HUMILITY

Abu Bakr was very kind and compassionate to his fellow believers. A very wealthy merchant, he always cared for the poor and the weak. He freed seven slaves before leaving Makkah, among them Bilal. He not only spent large amounts to buy their freedom he then took them into his own household and educated them.

During Abu Bakr's khilafah when times were diffacult, Bilal wanted to join the campaign heading towards Syria. Out of Abu Bakr's fondness for Bilal he said, "Oh Bilal, I did not think you would leave us under such circumstances. I wish you would stay here and help us in the diffacult times." Bilal replied, "If you had released me from bondage for the pleasure of Allah, the Most Exalted, then let me go to Him, but if you bought me for your own needs then keep me." Abu Bakr immediately gave him permission to leave.

HIS EXCELLENCE

Abu Bakr was also a poet before he became a Muslim. He was known for his exceptional recitation and his excellent memory of the long poems in which the Arabs took great pride. His recitation of the Qur'an was so beautiful that many people came to Islam simply after hearing him pray. The Quraysh tried to forbid his praying in the courtyard of his house in order to prevent the people from hearing him.

Bukhari narrates from Ibn 'Umar that, "In the time of the Prophet we were not recognising anyone higher than Abu Bakr as-Siddique, then 'Umar, then 'Uthman."

Bukhari also narrates from Muhammad ibn al-Hanafiya ('Ali's son), "I asked my father, 'Who are the best people after Allah's Apostle?' He said, 'Abu Bakr.' I asked, 'Who then?' He said, 'Then 'Umar.' I was afraid he would say 'Uthman next, so I said, 'Then you?' Sayidina 'Ali humbly replied, 'I am only an ordinary person.'"

He also related from 'Ali, "If you thought of something good to do, then Abu Bakr would have already done it."

It is also narrated by Bukhari that 'Ali said, "The best of this community after the Prophet are Abu Bakr and 'Umar. As for myself I am only an ordinary man among the Muslims."

What the Ka'aba may have looked like in the time of Abu Bakr. From the Madian Project

ABU BAKR'S HIDDEN GOOD DEEDS

No one could outdo Abu Bakr in good actions. Once, Sayyidina 'Umar decided to follow Abu Bakr to see where he went every day after the Fajr prayer. Most people went home to rest but Abu Bakr would disappear and return home later.

Without letting him see, 'Umar followed Abu Bakr as he made his way out of Medina. He followed him for quite a while until he saw Abu Bakr come to a small house in an isolated part of the countryside. Abu Bakr went in. Umar waited for a couple of hours until the sun began to get hot in the sky, and finally, Abu Bakr emerged and began to make his way home. Hidden out of sight, 'Umar waited until Abu Bakr passed and went to the small house. He knocked at the door and an old lady answered, she was blind and was surrounded by small children. 'Umar asked about the man who came each day and what he did and if she knew who it was. "No, I do not know who comes every day, but he cleans the house, grinds the flour, makes bread and prepares breakfast for us. I am a blind woman and am taking care of these orphans."

'Umar marvelled at this generous and kind action and he bade farewell to the lady.

Abu Bakr also would continue to milk the goats of the widows and orphans, which was a charitable act he did before he became khalifah. When he continued to do this even after he became khalifah, people questioned him about this, as he was busy with state affairs. Abu Bakr replied; "I would hate that the title khalifah would take a good characteristic from me, such that it would be said, 'He used to do something good until he became khalifah.'"

'Nus Nushirvan and the Two Owls'. 16th Century persian, ink, watercolour and gold leaf. Courtesy of the British Museum

THE BEST FRIEND OF THE PROPHET ﷺ

He was the best friend of the Prophet Muhammad ﷺ and they would love to be in each other's company. The Prophet ﷺ said, *"If I were to choose an intimate friend, other than Allah, I would choose Abu Bakr."*

Once, when the Prophet Muhammad ﷺ and Abu Bakr were praying at the Ka'aba, their praise of Allah reached the ears of the Quraysh, who became furious and angrily rushed at the Prophet ﷺ to try and harm him. Before they could reach their target, Abu Bakr, although a thin man, threw himself at the assailants. They beat Abu Bakr until he looked like a corpse and was unconscious. When the assailants left, Abu Bakr was brought to his house and lay there for a long time. Many thought he would die. As he opened his eyes, the first thing he asked was, "Where is Muhammad...where is the Prophet, is he okay?" The family, who were not yet Muslim, were angered and they left. Only his mother remained. She tried to get him to drink some water, but Abu Bakr said, "I will not eat or drink until I see Muhammad." His mother said, "You nearly died, and all you can think about is Muhammad!"

His mother went to get 'Umar al-Khattab's sister, who had secretly embraced Islam. When she arrived, she burst into tears and said, "What human can do this to a man?" They carried him to Muhammad ﷺ and when he saw him, he too began to cry and all the Muslims cried with him.

Many years later when he heard that the Prophet ﷺ had permsission from Allah to migrate to Medina, such was his love for the Prophet ﷺ, that he grew desperate and begged to accompany him, not able to think of anything else. When the Prophet ﷺ said yes, he cried tears of happiness according to Sayyidah 'Aisha.

17th Century Persian painting depicting the cave where the Prophet ﷺ hid with Abu Bakr

They went by night, carefully covering their tracks until they reached the famous cave where they stayed for three days. Abu Bakr's daughter, Asma, brought provisions and two camels for them at great risk. A search party of the unbelievers came very close to the cave but Allah made a spider weave a large web in front of the entrance and a dove made a nest so the Makkans did not discover them.

HIS APPEARANCE

The historian, Al-Tabari, records the following interaction between 'Aisha and her paternal nephew, 'Abdullah ibn 'Abdul-Rahman ibn Abi Bakr:

When she was in her howdah and saw a man from among the Arabs passing by, she said, "I have not seen a man more like Abu Bakr than this one."

We said to her, "Describe Abu Bakr."

She said, "A slight, white man, thin-bearded and bowed. His waist wrapper would not hold but would fall down around his loins. He had a lean face, sunken eyes, a bulging forehead, and trembling knuckles."

Referencing another source, Al-Tabari further describes him as being, "White mixed with yellowness, of good build, slight, bowed, thin, tall like a male palm tree, hook-nosed, lean-faced, sunken-eyed, thin-shanked, and strong-thighed. He used to dye himself with henna and black dye."

All acknowledged that he had a great presence about him.

ABU BAKR'S BET

Before betting was made unlawful, and although Abu Bakr was not a betting man, there was one bet he placed.

This happened when the Surah of 'Ar-Rum' (Rome) was revealed which predicted that the Persians would be defeated by the Romans within two to nine years. When this was revealed it seemed highly unlikely as the Persians were known to be strong and well-established with excellent armies and the Romans were at a time of weakness and their Empire was in decline.

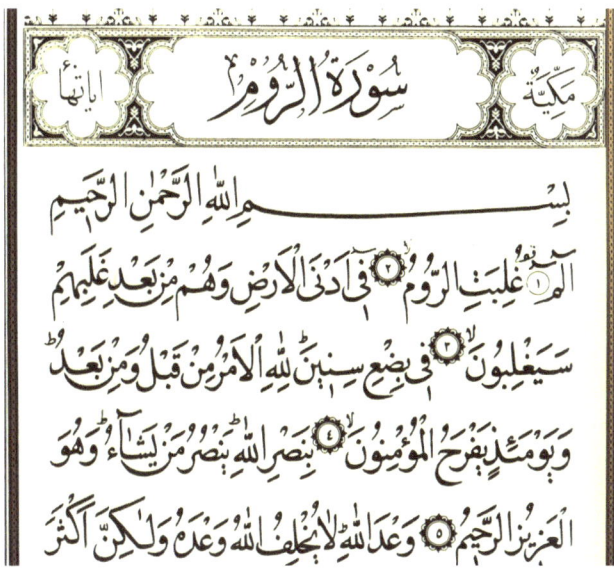

The beginning of Sura Ar-Rum from the Qur'an

"Alif, Lam, Mim. The Romans have been defeated in the land nearby, but after their defeat, they will themselves be victorious in a few years time. The affair is Allah's from beginning to end. On that day, the mu'minun will rejoice in Allah's help. He grants victory to whoever He wills. He is the Almighty, the Most Merciful." (Ar-Rum 30:1-2)

'Ubayy ibn Khalaf scoffed at this Surah in the Qur'an and said it was a lie, so Sayyidina Abu Bakr said, "O enemy of Allah! You are a liar, I am willing to bet on this issue that in case the Christians would not overcome the Persians in three years' time, I will give you ten camels, and if they did overcome, then you will have to give me ten camels".

After saying that, Abu Bakr went to the Holy Prophet ﷺ and narrated the episode. The Holy Prophet ﷺ replied and said to him to fix the time of nine years, because Qur'an has used the word *bid' sinin* (a few years) under which the time limit could be anything between three to nine years. Therefore, the Holy Prophet ﷺ asked Abu Bakr to go back and say that he would bet for hundred camels instead of ten, but the time limit would be nine (and according to some other reports, seven) years and not three. Abu Bakr followed the instructions of the Holy Prophet ﷺ and 'Ubayy Ibn Khalaf agreed on the new terms.

Abu Bakr had no doubt about the revelation that the Prophet ﷺ had just received.

After two years had passed, the possibility of the Romans defeating the Persians was looking even more unlikely but still, Abu Bakr did not falter, such was the trust he had in the holy words of the Qur'an.

'Ubayy ibn Khalaf must have scoffed at Abu Bakr many times and looked forward to when he would receive one hundred camels, which in those days was a fortune. However, 'Ubayy ibn

Khalaf did not live long enough to see the outcome of the bet, so his son took the bet over.

It was around the time of the Battle of Badr when the prediction came true. On March 25, 624, Heraclius left Constantinople with an army of no more than 40,000, marched through Persia, capturing important cities and towns until he reached Ganzaka where he met Khosrow's army of similar size and defeated them. Allah's ﷻ Words indeed came true.

'Ubayy ibn Khalaf's son handed over the one hundred camels to Abu Bakr who then brought them to the Holy Prophet ﷺ who asked him to give the camels away in charity.

Abu Bakr as Khalifah

The Prophet Muhammad ﷺ had introduced a whole new way of life, with justice and social laws that gave everyone their rights, but after the Prophet ﷺ died, there was much unrest among the people. Abu Bakr had to act swiftly or everything that the Prophet ﷺ had established would dissolve and oppression would return. Abu Bakr was determined to maintain the excellent social structures put in place by the Prophet Muhammad ﷺ and to follow the new laws, exactly as the Prophet ﷺ had done. This brought much relief to those who had, before Islam, been oppressed or poor and hungry, and had valid fears that after the Prophet's ﷺ death, things would go back to the old ways.

Abu Bakr did indeed have a huge task on his hands. It was essential to continue the Bayt al-Mal (Social Fund) and to have money for the poor, the orphans, the widows and other important social services. For this to continue, everyone who was obliged needed to give *zakat* (charity), otherwise, the social structures would collapse. Of course, issues with money are often the first things people will disagree about and some of the tribes stopped paying *zakat*.

TEACHING ISLAM

An essential part of Abu Bakr's plan for establishing Islam and the khalifah, was to send many envoys to all the surrounding tribes and to the tribes in northern Arabia, to teach them more about Islam. In those days, few people could read or write, so they learned about Islam through oral narrations of hadith and learning from scholars and those who knew the Prophet ﷺ. One person would learn from another and then pass on what they knew to others. Many people converted to Islam in this fashion. Tribes who wanted to know more about Islam would send envoys to Medina, where most of the Companions of the Prophet ﷺ lived.

It may have been more difficult for rulers and emperors themselves to accept Islam, even if they felt it to be true, as they were in high positions of power. Islam means 'to submit' and the greater the pride, the harder it is to submit.

"Muhammad and Abu Bakr are welcomed by Umm Ma 'badah 's tribe," from a 16th-century illuminated manuscript.

THE BAYT AL-MAL

The Bayt al-Mal was the public treasury that dealt with the revenues and all other economic matters of the state. In the time of the Prophet ﷺ the Bayt al-Mal was used for a large variety of government purposes: looking after the poor, building new buildings, equipping the army, sending envoys etc. Generally, whatever revenues or other amounts were received from *zakat, sadaqa* or other sources were distributed immediately.

SPIRITUAL LEADER OF THE MUSLIMS

By Hana Horack-Elyafi

As the khalifah of Islam, Abu Bakr not only had the responsibility of the wordly welfare of the *Ummah* or Muslim community, but was also responsible for the spiritual guidance of the Ummah. This included all inner and outer forms of the religion as he had been taught by the Prophet Muhammad ﷺ.

Abu Bakr as-Siddique, as 'the mirror of the Prophet', continued to teach the Companions about the inner strugle or, Jihad of the Heart. This is how the Companions and sincere Muslims perfect their character as the Prophet ﷺ said "I have come to perfect good character." (Malik). This includes removing all traces of hypocrisy, oppression and negative characteristics of the blameworthy ego. The person can then be described as someone who has purified their soul, as mentioned in Qur'an,

"Allah loves those who are constantly repentant and loves those who purify themselves." (Al Baqara 2:222)

After Fajr prayer, Abu Bakr would give a spiritual talk, as the Prophet ﷺ had done, teaching the ways of Tasawwuf, the purification of the heart.

Abu Bakr said, *"Whoever has tasted the pristine love of Allah is preoccupied away from worldly pursuits..."*

PRESERVATION OF THE QUR'AN

Abu Bakr also made the first steps in preserving the Qur'an in written form. It is said that after the victory over Musaylimah in the Battle of Yamama in 632, 'Umar saw that some five hundred of the Muslims who had memorised the Qur'an had been killed. After this terrible event, and fearing that the Qur'an may become lost or corrupted, 'Umar pleaded with Abu Bakr to authorise the compilation and preservation of the scriptures in written format, even though this was not something the Prophet ﷺ had ordered.

"How can we do that which the Messenger of Allah ﷺ, did not himself do?" Abu Bakr worried. He eventually relented and appointed Zayd ibn Thabit, who had previously served as Prophet Muhammad's ﷺ secretary, the task of gathering the verses which were scattered in various places. The fragments were recovered from every quarter, including from the ribs of palm branches, scraps of leather, stone tablets, and "from the hearts of men". The collected work was copied onto parchment and checked by comparison with Qur'an memorisers.

This was then presented to Abu Bakr, who passed it to 'Umar, who then passed it to his daughter Hafsa, who had been one of the blessed wives of Muhammad ﷺ. It was this volume,

Fragments of Qur'an - Surah al-Anbiya 21:36-42. Ashmolean Museum, University of Oxford. Surah al-Anbiya' (The Prophets), 21:36-42; 8th/2nd

borrowed from Hafsa, which formed the basis of 'Uthman's legendary prototype, which became the definitive text of the Qur'an. All later editions are derived from this original copy.

Conflicts and Problems

Almost as soon as Abu Bakr assumed the khalifah, reports came back to him about a number of serious issues:

Muslayma the Liar by Hana Horack-Elyafi

REBEL TRIBES

After the death of the Prophet ﷺ, some rebels said that they did not recognise Abu Bakr as the new khalifah. They said that their allegiance was to the Prophet Muhammad ﷺ and they did not owe anything to Abu Bakr as-Siddique. In fact, they saw the death of the Prophet ﷺ as an opportunity to take over Medina.

They could not yet see how righteous and well-guided a leader Abu Bakr was to become. Like a star that we cannot see when the sun is out, Abu Bakr had put himself in the shadow of the Prophet ﷺ, to absorb every word and teaching. So when the sun did set on the life of the Prophet ﷺ in this world, it took a little while, not too long, before the leadership of Abu Bakr began to shine forth.

Other tribes wanted to continue with Islam but not pay the zakat on their extra wealth and wanted to adjust the rules to suit themselves.

Other tribes decided to leave Islam and were known as the apostate tribes.

FALSE PROPHETS

In addition to this, there were some leaders of various tribes who proclaimed themselves prophets. They took some of the things they liked in Islam and took out the things they didn't like. The most famous was Musaylimah the Liar from the Banu Hanifa tribe who were the most troublesome tribe to the Prophet ﷺ. The Banu Hanifa laughed about Musaylimah, but supported him because he was from them. There was also Tulayha from the Banu Asad ibn Khuzaymah tribe as well as the false prophetess, Sajah, from the Banu Taghlib from Iraq.

Musaylimah the Liar, encouraged people to eat pork and drink wine, taught three daily prayers, facing any direction, to fast Ramadan at night, rather than during the day and not to perform circumcision. He was a skilled magician who was said to be able to put an egg in a bottle and cut feathers off a bird, stick them back on and it would fly again! He claimed that Muhammad ﷺ gave him these powers and also a share of the prophecy. He was a brutal, vicious murderer who would crucify people for not following him. In fact, he slaughtered entire caravans if they were against him. Quite a few people started to follow him out of fear. He would write his own verses, mainly describing his tribe as superior to the Quraysh and praising the virtues of food.

During the time of the Prophet ﷺ, Musaylimah had proposed to share power over Arabia with Muhammad ﷺ. In late 10 Hijri, he wrote to Muhammad ﷺ,

"From Musaylimah, Messenger of God, to Muhammad, Messenger of God. Salutations to you. I have been given a share with you in this matter. Half the Earth belongs to us and a half to the Quraysh. But the Quraysh are people who transgress."

Prophet Muhammad ﷺ replied,

"From Muhammad, the Messenger of God, to Musaylimah, the Arch-Liar. Peace be upon him who follows (God's) guidance. Now then, surely the Earth belongs to God, Who bequeaths it to whom He will amongst His servants. The ultimate issue is to the God-fearing."

BYZANTINES AND PERSIANS

There were also troubles on the northern borders with the Byzantines (Eastern Roman Empire) as well as the Persians to the northeast. They heard of the Prophet's ﷺ death and the problems within Arabia. They knew that if Arabia was becoming divided, it could be within their grasp.

Xerxes I, also known as Xerxes the Great, was a 5th century Achaemenid king of the Persian empire. He is best known for leading the massive invasion of Greece, marked by the battles of Thermopylae, Salamis and Plataea.

FIVE PART PLAN

Abu Bakr had to think very carefully about what to do to sort out all five issues as soon as possible. He needed to:

Protect Medina.

Establish unity and peace among the Arab tribes.

Sort out the false prophets.

Divide up the army in a sensible way, but not spread it too thin on any front.

Fortify the northern front againt the Byzantines and Persians.

TACTICAL DILEMMA

Abu Bakr had a difficult decision on his hands, should he follow the Prophet's ﷺ orders to take 3000 men back to the Byzantium borders or defend Medina against the rebels who were threatening to take over?

There were risks in not going to the Byzantium borders because Muslims were being attacked and there were rebellions building.

Outside Medina the rebel tribes were getting close - 'Umar advised to stay and fight the rebels first to secure Medina.

Abu Bakr thought about it but decided to continue with the order of the Prophet ﷺ. On June 26th 632, 11 A.H., the army moved out and marched to Tabuk under the great commander Usama ibn Zayd.

Before they left, Abu Bakr reminded them of the orders of the Prophet ﷺ in battle:

"See that you avoid treachery and do what's right. Do not mutilate anyone. You should not kill children, women or old men. Do not injure the date palm. Do not cut down any tree wherein there is food for men and beasts. Do not slay the flocks of herds of camels save for needful sustenance. You may eat the meat that the men of the land may bring to you in their vessels, mentioning the name of Allah. Do not molest the monks in the churches, and leave them to themselves. Now march forward in the name of Allah. Fulfil the mission entrusted to you. May Allah protect you from sword and pestilence!"

Ahead of the army, Usama sent messengers to teach and invite people to peaceful agreements before the main army arrived. As a direct result of his operations, several rebel tribes resubmitted to Medinan rule and they re-accepted Islam.

Usama next marched to Mu'tah, in the north of Arabia, and engaged the Christian Arabs of the tribes of Banu Kalb and the Hasanids in a small battle. Then he returned to Medina, bringing with him a large number of captives and a considerable amount of wealth, part of which comprised the spoils of war and jizya (non-Muslim taxation) of the re-conquered tribes.

WHAT WAS ABU BAKR LIKE ON THE BATTLEFIELD?

Although a quiet and a gentle person he was also first on the battlefield. He supported the Holy Prophet ﷺ in all of his campaigns both with his sword and with his counsel. When others failed or deserted the army, he remained at the side of his beloved Prophet ﷺ. It is stated that once 'Ali asked his companions whom they considered to be the bravest. They replied that 'Ali was the bravest. But he answered, "No, Abu Bakr is the bravest. On the day of the Battle of Badr when there was no one to stand guard where the Holy Prophet ﷺ prayed, Abu Bakr stood with his sword and did not allow the enemy to come near."

Battle of Badr in which Abu Bakr took part, Il-Khanid: Tabriz Khalili

An Ottoman 'kilij' sword set with corals

THE REBEL TRIBES AND THE DEFENCE OF MEDINA

Most of the rebels were positioned in two towns, Abraq, 72 miles to the northeast, and Dhu Qissa, 24 miles east of Medina. These concentrations consisted of the tribes of Banu Ghatafan, the Hawazin, and the Tayy. Abu Bakr sent envoys to all the enemy tribes, calling upon them to remain loyal to Islam and continue to pay their zakat.

However, a week or two after the departure of Usama's army, the rebel tribes surrounded Medina, knowing that there were few fighting forces in the city. Meanwhile, Tulayha, one of the self-proclaimed prophets, joined the rebels at Dhu Qissa. In the third week of July 11, 632 (11 A.H.), the apostate army moved from Dhu Qissa to Dhu Hussa, from where they prepared to launch an attack on Medina.

Abu Bakr received intelligence of the rebel movements and immediately prepared for the defence of Medina. As Usama's army was elsewhere, Abu Bakr scraped together a fighting force mainly from the clan of Muhammad ﷺ, the Banu Hashim. The army had some of the original Companions, like Talha ibn Ubaydullah and Zubayr ibn al-

Awam, who would later (in the 640s) conquer Egypt. Each of them was appointed commander of one-third of the newly organised force. Before the apostates had time to attack, Abu Bakr launched his army against their outposts and drove them back to Dhu Hussa. (See map overleaf).

Arabs usually employed camels in battle. Caravan by E. Curry 2001

PROBLEMS WITH CAMELS AT DHU QISSA

The following day, Abu Bakr intended to march from Medina with his forces and moved towards Dhu Hussa but had a few problems. He needed camels for his army but the best ones were all at the Byzantine border with Usama. So Abu Bakr had to use pack animals which were untrained for battle. This meant that when Hibal, the rebel commander at Dhu Hussa, launched a surprise attack from the hills, the camels bolted. As a result, the Muslims retreated to Medina, and the rebels recaptured the outposts that they had lost a few days earlier. Back in Medina, Abu Bakr regrouped and attacked the rebels during the night, taking them by surprise. The rebels retreated from Dhu Hussa to Dhu Qissa. The following morning, Abu Bakr led his army to Dhu Qissa, and defeated the rebel tribes, capturing Dhu Qissa on 1 August 632 (11 A.H.)

The defeated rebel tribes then retreated further to Abraq, where more clansmen of the Ghatafan, the Hawazin, and the Tayy were gathered. Abu Bakr left a residual force under the command of An-Nu'man ibn Muqarin at Dhu Qissa and returned with his main army to Medina.

USAMA'S ARMY RETURNS

Usama's army returned and was welcomed back to Medina with all the captives and the wealth after their successes at the Byzantium border. Abu Bakr then ordered him and the men to rest and recover for the next operations.

Meanwhile, in the second week of August, 632, Abu Bakr travelled with his army to Dhu Qissa, joined with ibn Muqarin's remaining forces and together they moved to Abraq, where the rebels had gathered, and defeated them. The remaining rebels retreated to Buzakha, where Tulayha, the false prophet, had positioned himself with his army from Samira.

In the fourth week of August, 632, Abu Bakr gathered all all available fighting forces at Dhu Qissa. There he planned his strategy, in what would later be called the Campaign of Apostasy or the Ridda Wars, to deal with the various enemies who occupied the rest of Arabia.

He had so far succeeded in defeating the rebel tribes that were trying to take over Medina and this sent a message to the enemies that Abu Bakr was indeed in control and the Khalifah from Medina was to be taken seriously.

Abu Bakr now had a secure base from which he could conduct the major campaign that lay ahead.

WHAT IS JIZYA?

Like zakat, which is the tax of 2.5% of the extra wealth that most Muslims have to pay, the jizya is specifically for non-Muslims. The amount would vary in different khalifates but used to start at one dirham per year (4.234 grams of gold). The amount also varied according to income. Sayyidina 'Umar set the rate at four dirhams for the wealthy, two for the middle class and one for the working class. The money would then go to the Bayt al-Mal, the government treasury for social care, administration and other government expenses. For reference, one dinar was approximately equivalent to two to three days of family expenditure. In return, the Muslim state would protect and care for its members, including negotiating the release of any of them from capture. The non-Muslims are to receive the same advantages as the Muslims. It is also stated that it needs to be collected with leniency and politeness.

Not everyone had to pay it. Those exempt were: women, children, the elderly, the disabled, the ill, both physically and mentally, monks, hermits and slaves. Also exempt, were those who could not afford to pay.

RIDDA WARS

632-633 C.E. (11-12 A.H)

The Khalifah distributed the available manpower among eleven units, each under its own commander, and bearing its own standard. While some commanders were given immediate missions, other missions were to be launched later. Abu Bakr's plan was first to clear west-central Arabia (the area nearest to Medina), then tackle Malik bin Nuwayra, and finally concentrate his forces against the most dangerous and powerful enemy: the self-proclaimed prophet Musaylima.

The commanders and their assigned objectives were:

Khalid ibn Walid*: Move against Tulayha bin Khuwaylid al-Asadi from the Asad Tribe at Buzaakhah, then Malik ibn Nuwaira, at Butah.

Ikrimah ibn Abi-Jahl*: Confront Musaylima at Yamamah but not engage until more forces arrive.

'Amr ibn al-Aas*: Quell the apostate tribes of Quza'a and Wadi'a in the area of Tabuk and Daumat al-Jandal.

Shurahbil ibn Hasana*: Follow Ikrimah and await the Khalifah's instructions.

Khalid bin Sa'eed*: Quell the apostate tribes on the Syrian frontier.

Turayfa bin Hajiz*: Quell the apostate tribes of Hawazin and Bani Sulaym in the area east of Medina and Makkah.

'Ala ibn al-Hadhrami*: Quell the apostates in Bahrain.

Arfaja bin Harthama*: Quell the apostates in Mahra.

Hudhayfa bin Mihsan*: Quell the apostates in Oman.

Muhajir bin Abi Umayyah*: Quell the apostates in Yemen.

Suwayd bin Muqaran*: Quell the apostates in the coastal area north of Yemen.

As soon as the units were organised, Khalid* marched off, to be followed a little later by Ikrimah and 'Amr ibn al-As*. The other units were held back by the Khalifah and dispatched weeks and even months later, according to the progress of Khalid's operations against the worst of enemy opposition.

Before the various units left, however, envoys were sent by Abu Bakr* to all apostate tribes in a final attempt to induce them to submit.

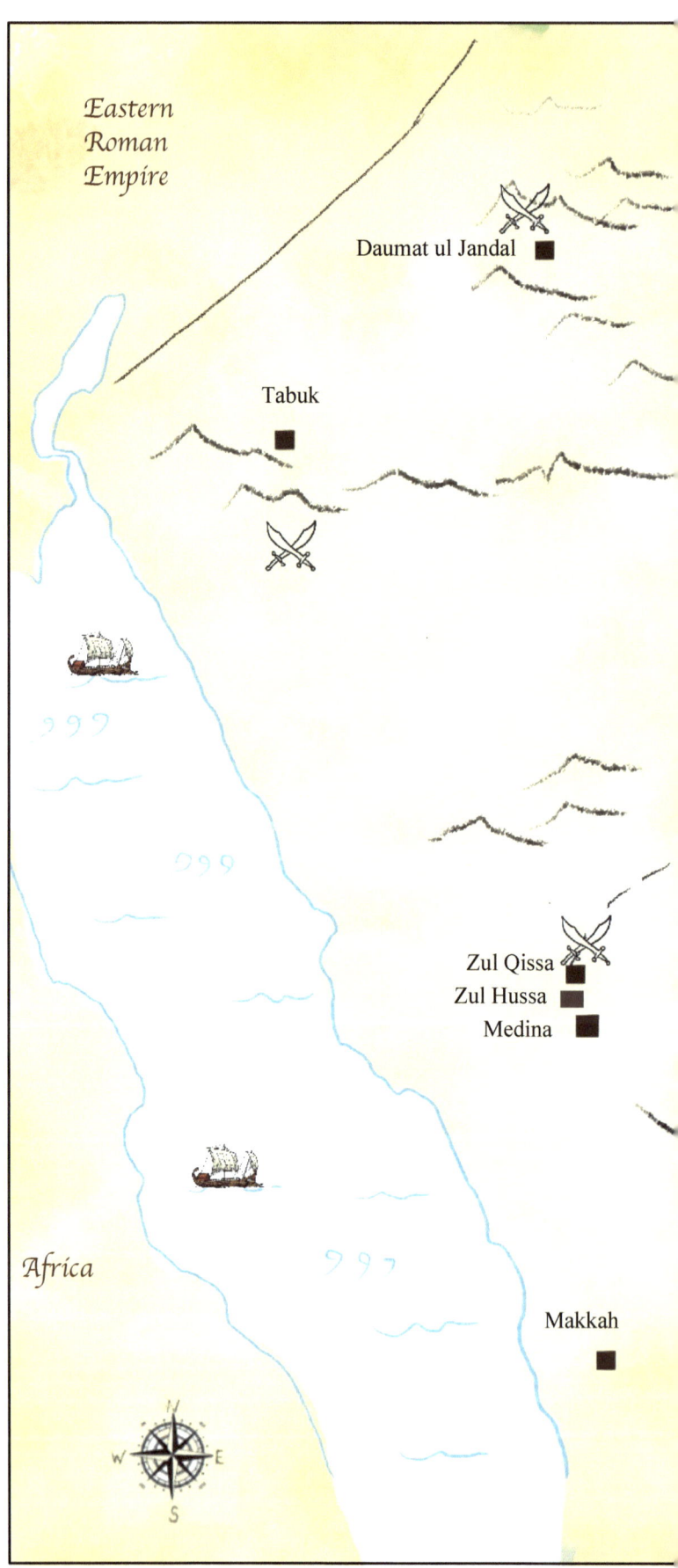

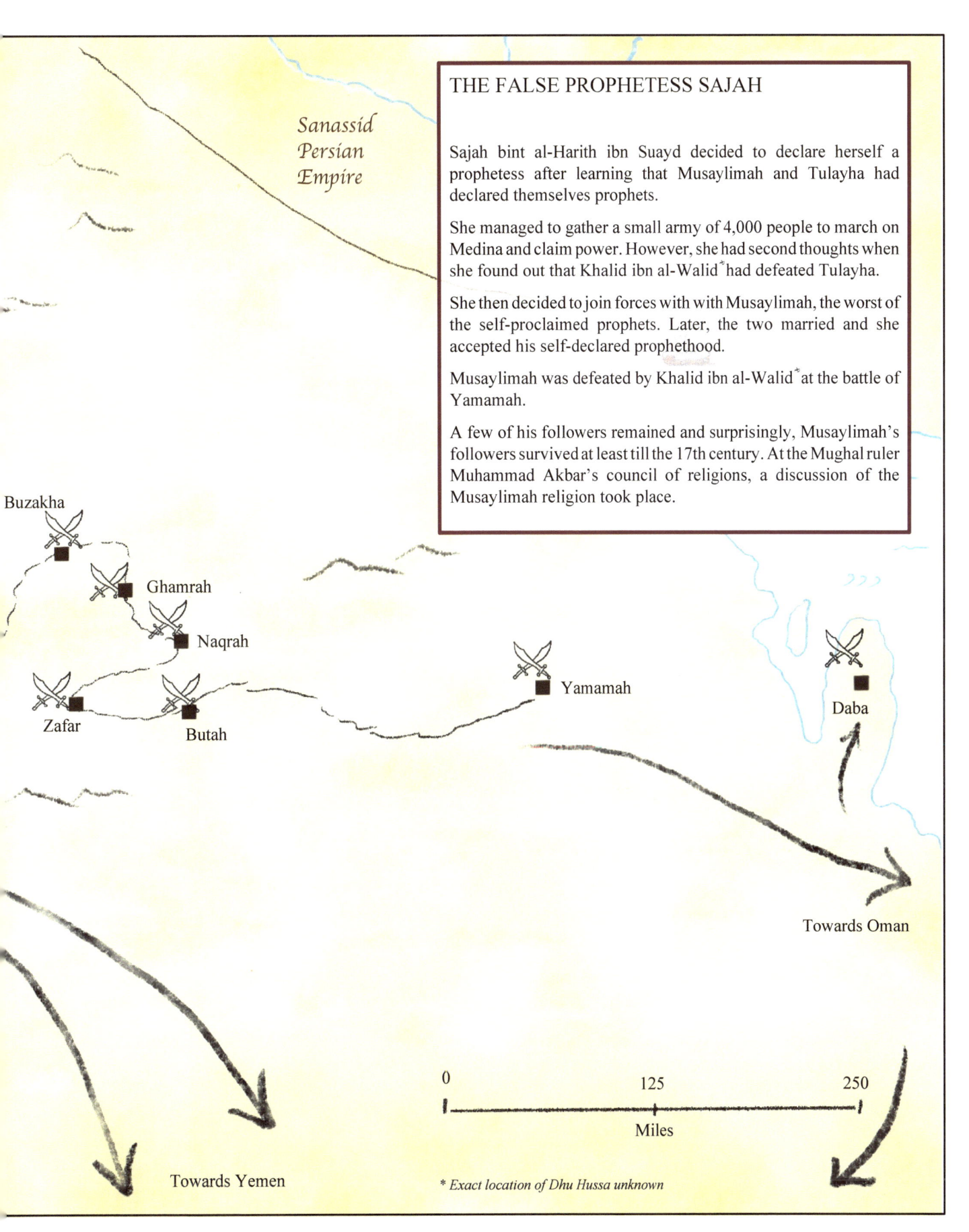

Sanassid Persian Empire

THE FALSE PROPHETESS SAJAH

Sajah bint al-Harith ibn Suayd decided to declare herself a prophetess after learning that Musaylimah and Tulayha had declared themselves prophets.

She managed to gather a small army of 4,000 people to march on Medina and claim power. However, she had second thoughts when she found out that Khalid ibn al-Walid* had defeated Tulayha.

She then decided to join forces with with Musaylimah, the worst of the self-proclaimed prophets. Later, the two married and she accepted his self-declared prophethood.

Musaylimah was defeated by Khalid ibn al-Walid* at the battle of Yamamah.

A few of his followers remained and surprisingly, Musaylimah's followers survived at least till the 17th century. At the Mughal ruler Muhammad Akbar's council of religions, a discussion of the Musaylimah religion took place.

Buzakha

Ghamrah

Naqrah

Zafar

Butah

Yamamah

Daba

Towards Oman

Towards Yemen

0   125   250
Miles

* Exact location of Dhu Hussa unknown

BATTLE OF YAMAMAH

632 (Rajab/Shaaban 11 A.H)

Plain of Aqraba - Against Musaylimah the Liar

A Persian painting of the famous battle inside the garden wall at Yamamah.

Abu Bakr * commanded Ikrimah * to camp near Musaylimah's stronghold whose numbers were surprisingly large - up to 40,000 men were reported. For this reason, Abu Bakr * told Ikrimah * to stay put and not attack until reinforcements arrived, in particular to wait for Khalid ibn Walid *. The presence of Ikrimah * was enough to stop Musaylimah from advancing towards Medina.

Ikrimah * was a fearless man and a forceful general, but he lacked Khalid's * cool judgement and patience. Even before Shurahbil's * unit arrived in just a matter of days, Ikrimah * gave the command to attack and was, unfortunately, defeated by Musaylimah's army.

He wrote to Abu Bakr * and gave him a complete account of his actions. Abu Bakr * was both pained and angered by the rashness of Ikrimah * and his disobedience to the orders given to him. Abu Bakr * ordered him to march to Mahra to help Arfaja * and thereafter go to Yemen to help Muhajir. Shurahbil * remained in the region of Yamamah. To ensure that he did not fall into the error of Ikrimah, Abu Bakr wrote to him, "Stay where you are and await further instructions."

The Khalifa * wrote to Shurahbil * to work under Khalid ibn al-Walid's * command who had been ordered to march to Yamamah. A few days before Khalid's * arrival, Shurahbil * gave in to the same temptation as Ikrimah: he advanced and clashed with Musaylimah and was also defeated. These victories increased confidence among Musaylimah's followers and created an aura of invincibility around him. His fortress was known as 'The Garden of Death' (Hadeeqat al-Mawt), it was superbly armed and inaccessible.

Finally, Khalid's * army arrived and immediately attacked Musaylimah, terrible carnage ensued, such was the intensity of the fighting. Blood ran down a gully which is still known as the Gully of Blood (Shuayb ad-Dam). The heavy fighting of that day was indecisive and both sides retired to rest for the night.

The next phase, known as The Second Strike of the Muslims, is a source of legend due to the heroism of Al-Bara ibn Malik. He was the older brother of Anas ibn Malik (narrator of 278 Hadiths) whose life he saved in the Battle of Tustar. Al-Bara * was extremely short and thin, the Companions used to degrade him until the Prophet ﷺ gave him as the example of those dishevelled, unkempt and dusty people whose oath is immediately accepted by Allah. All stories about him relate to his skill in battles and he would single-handedly kill so many more people in battles than the other soldiers that it caused problems in the division of booty. When 'Umar ibn al-Khattab * became khalifah, he warned his commanders not to make Al-Bara * a general because his courage would have led whole battalions to follow him to death.

There were 20,000 enemy soldiers in the impenetrable fortress and Al-Bara * said to Khalid ibn Walid, "Strap me to a shield and catapult me inside, I'll fight my way through and open the gate."

Khalid * and the other Muslims were shocked but he insisted, "O Muslims, throw me at them!" Eventually, they agreed and catapulted him into the Garden of Death. His fall was broken by the surprised enemy soldiers and he was able to fight through and kill guards of the gate to let the Muslims in.

After opening the gates he went in search of Musaylimah's personal bodyguard, a gigantic man who was known as the most dangerous of his fighters. Musaylimah was a coward and led the battle from the back, hiding. Al-Bara * walked up to the bodyguard, who thought it was a joke when he saw this small, wounded man approaching. Al-Bara * defeated the bodyguard, which gave the opening for Wahshi ibn Harb's * to kill Musaylimah with the same spear that he had used to kill Hamza, of which he said, "I killed the best of people with this spear and I killed the worst of people with it. This is my repentance to Allah."

Wahshi's * spear pierced the stomach of Musaylimah while Abu Dujana * cut off his head. Now, with the hand-to-hand fighting in close quarters, which the Muslim warriors excelled at, they quickly defeated the rest of Musaylimah's army.

After the battle and out of respect and gratitude to Al-Bara, Khalid ibn Walid * stayed with him for a whole month, nursing him back to health. Al-Bara * had received 80 wounds in this battle, 40 from arrows and 40 from the sword. Khalid * attributed the victory at Al-Yamamah to Al-Bara *.

This battle ended the Ridda wars.

Abu Bakr was now seen as a leader in his own right, one who was prepared to fight alongside his army, and not someone to alter or dilute the precious messages and rules of Islam. The Arab tribes now respected his leadership and the rule from Medina. The tribes sent envoys to renew their bayat and to pay the *zakat*.

MUSLIM EXPANSION UNDER ABU BAKR

It was essential to secure the borders of Arabia against attacks from other empires. There had been a history of threats and attacks from the Persian and Byzantine empires, both of whom stood on the northern borders of Arabia. There was Persia to the east and Byzantium to the west. (See map overleaf)

Abu Bakr* hoped that by attacking Iraq, where the Persians were, and Syria, where the Romans were, he might remove the danger from these borders.

He knew that regions governed by the Persians and Romans were highly taxed; Abu Bakr* believed that these regions might be persuaded to help the Muslims, who in return, would help them to be free of the high taxes.

Persian warrior in line, stone carving Sassanid Empire 5th century B.C..

PERSIAN EMPIRE

The Persian Empire is also known more specifically as the Sassanid Dynasty, as it was this family that ruled for many years. This rule had begun about 400 years earlier and covered a large area including what we now know as Iran and Iraq as well as some eastern areas of Arabia.

A few years before, the Prophet ﷺ had sent a letter of invitation to Islam to the Persian Emperor, Khosrow the II. Khosroe had torn the Prophet's ﷺ letter into little pieces. Enraged by the letter, he ordered his ally, the tribal leader of Yemen, to capture Muhammad ﷺ and kill him. However, when the leader of Yemen arrived in Medina and met the Prophet ﷺ, he accepted Islam and then dedicated Yemen to the Prophet ﷺ.

The Prophet ﷺ had predicted that the Persian Empire would break into pieces, just as the letter had been ripped apart, and it was not too long before this came to pass.

At the time, the Sassanid Dynasty was on the decline after constant wars with the Byzantine Romans. There was much treachery and backstabbing in the Persian court; an emperor might not last in power more than a few days before being killed by another family member wanting the throne. In the time of Abu Bakr's* khalifat, Yazdegerd III, only eight years old, was appointed. Yazdegerd III, being a child, lacked any experience and did not see a need to rebuild the depleted army.

A mosaic of glazed bricks from a palace of Darius I or Xerxes I (5th century BC), Achaemenid empire.

VICTORIES IN PERSIA

633 C.E. (12 A.H.)

Even though the Persian Empire was in decline, they were still a force to be reckoned with. To ensure victory, Abu Bakr made two decisions concerning the attack on Persia: first, the invading army would consist entirely of volunteers; and second, to put his best general, Khalid ibn al-Walid*, in command.

Around the third week of March 633 (first week of Muharram, 12th A.H.) Khalid set out from Al-Yamama with an army of 10,000. He met tribal chiefs along the way, who joined him, swelling his ranks to 18,000.

Upon arriving in Iraq, the first thing Khalid did was to send invitations to Islam to every governor and deputy who ruled the provinces and the rulers of the cities.

In all cases, they did not receive a friendly welcome.

The Persian court, already disturbed by internal problems, was thrown into chaos. After resting his armies in June, Khalid laid siege to the city of Al-Anbar, which surrendered in July. Khalid then moved towards the south and conquered the city of Ayn at-Tamr in the last week of July. At this point, most of what is now Iraq was under Islamic control.

Thse devastating defeats ended Persian control of those lands and left the capital, Ctesiphon, vulnerable. Before attacking Ctesiphon, as he did not have Abu Bakr's order for this, Khalid decided to eliminate all Persian forces in the south and west.

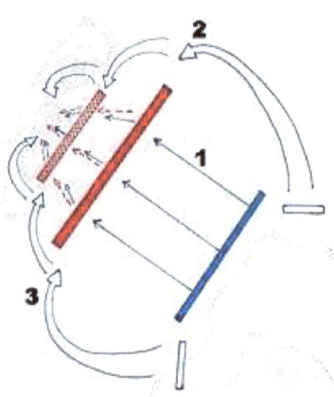

The double envelope manoeuvre used by Khalid Ibn Walid at the Battle of Walaja.*

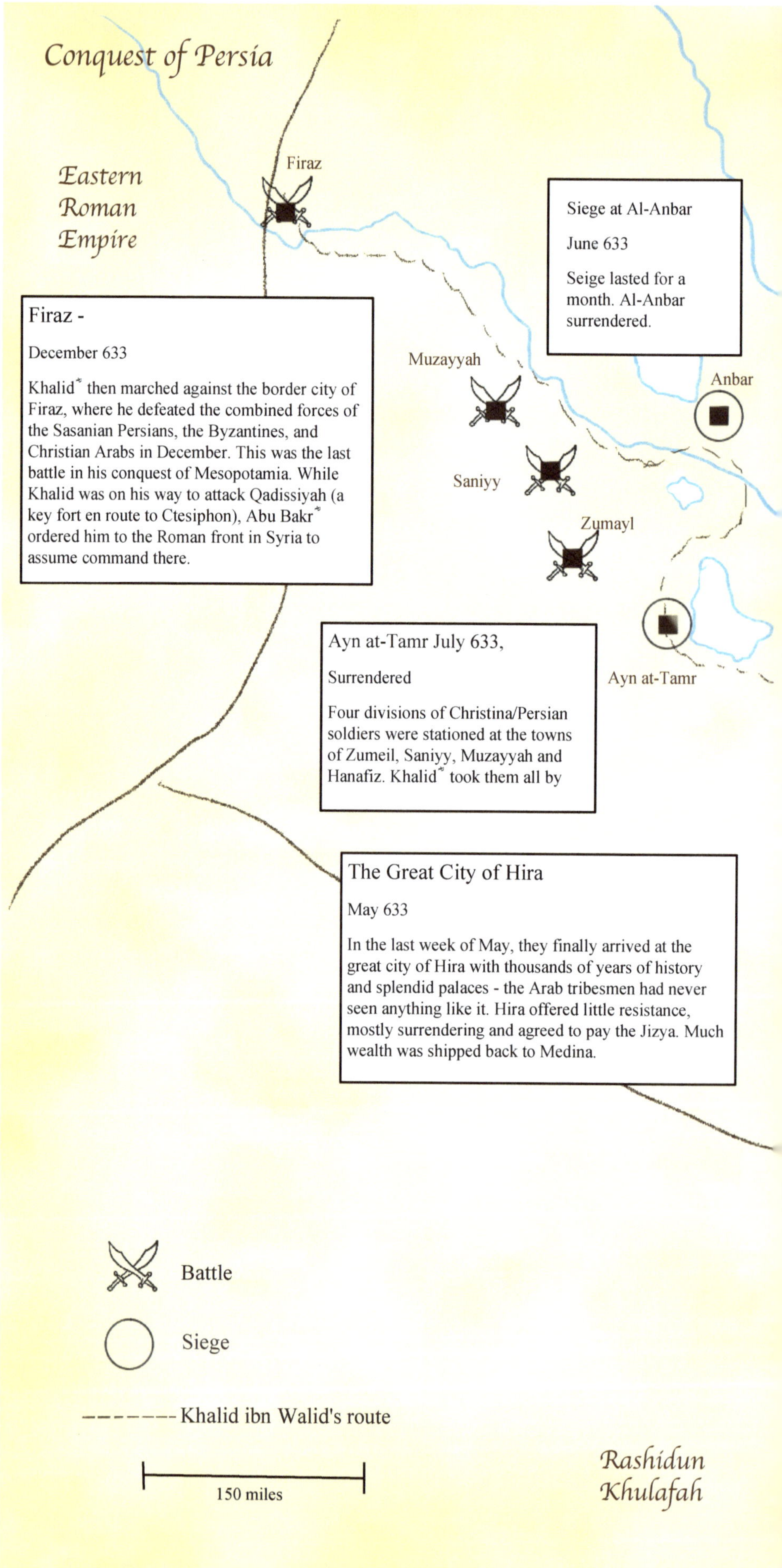

Conquest of Persia

Eastern
Roman
Empire

Firaz

Siege at Al-Anbar

June 633

Seige lasted for a month. Al-Anbar surrendered.

Muzayyah

Anbar

Firaz -

December 633

Khalid* then marched against the border city of Firaz, where he defeated the combined forces of the Sasanian Persians, the Byzantines, and Christian Arabs in December. This was the last battle in his conquest of Mesopotamia. While Khalid was on his way to attack Qadissiyah (a key fort en route to Ctesiphon), Abu Bakr* ordered him to the Roman front in Syria to assume command there.

Saniyy

Zumayl

Ayn at-Tamr July 633,

Surrendered

Four divisions of Christina/Persian soldiers were stationed at the towns of Zumeil, Saniyy, Muzayyah and Hanafiz. Khalid* took them all by

Ayn at-Tamr

The Great City of Hira

May 633

In the last week of May, they finally arrived at the great city of Hira with thousands of years of history and splendid palaces - the Arab tribesmen had never seen anything like it. Hira offered little resistance, mostly surrendering and agreed to pay the Jizya. Much wealth was shipped back to Medina.

⚔ Battle

◯ Siege

------- Khalid ibn Walid's route

150 miles

Rashidun Khulafah

KHALID'S* INVITATION TO ISLAM TO THE PERSIANS

"In the Name of Allah, the Most Compassionate and Merciful. Khalid ibn Walid sent this message to the satraps of Persia. Peace will be upon him who follows the guidance. All praise and thanks be to Allah who disperses your power and thwarts your deceitful plots. On the one hand, he who performs our prayers facing the direction of our Qiblah to face the sacred Mosque in Makkah and eats our slaughtered animals is a Muslim. He has the same rights and duties that we have. On the other hand, if you do not want to embrace Islam, then as soon as you recieve this message, send over the jizya and I give you my word that I will respect and honor this covenant. But if you do not agree to either choice, then, by Allah, I will send to you people who crave death as much as you crave life."

Baghdad

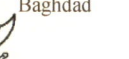

Ctesiphon

Sassanid Persian Empire

The Battle of Walaja

May 633

The following month where Khalid ibn Walid* successfully used a double envelopment maneuver. He positioned a contingent of cavalry to wait around the side of the mountain and other troops were positioned out of sight on each side. The main army engaged the Persians but then feigned defeat and backed up towards the hills where the reinforcements were waiting. The Persians thought that they were gaining the advantage but were then surrounded, with the cavalry attacking from behind and the troops on either side, so were defeated.

Hira

Ullais

Walaja

Mazar

The Battle of Chains

April 633

Upon receiving Khalid's* message, the governor of Kazimah sent an army in reply. The Governor himself had a duel with Khalid* and the governor was beheaded. It was called the Battle of the Chains because the Persians had a strange military strategy of chaining themselves together. Perhaps to make one, invincible army or to prevent men from running if the battle was going against them. Of course, this did not always work out very well, as once men were killed or injured, they had to be dragged around and the army could only move slowly.

The Battle of Ullais

May 633

Fought in mid-May. Found against a Christian tribe. Again, he invited them to Islam before the battle began.

So far, the Persians had lost hundreds of square miles of territory and some of their best generals.

The Battle of the River

April 633

Fought in the third week of April between Mazar and Uballa; Persians had brought a much larger force but Khalid ibn Walid's* forces were much faster and mobile and they struck before the others even formed ranks.

Uballa

Hufair

Kazimah

Conquest of the Levant

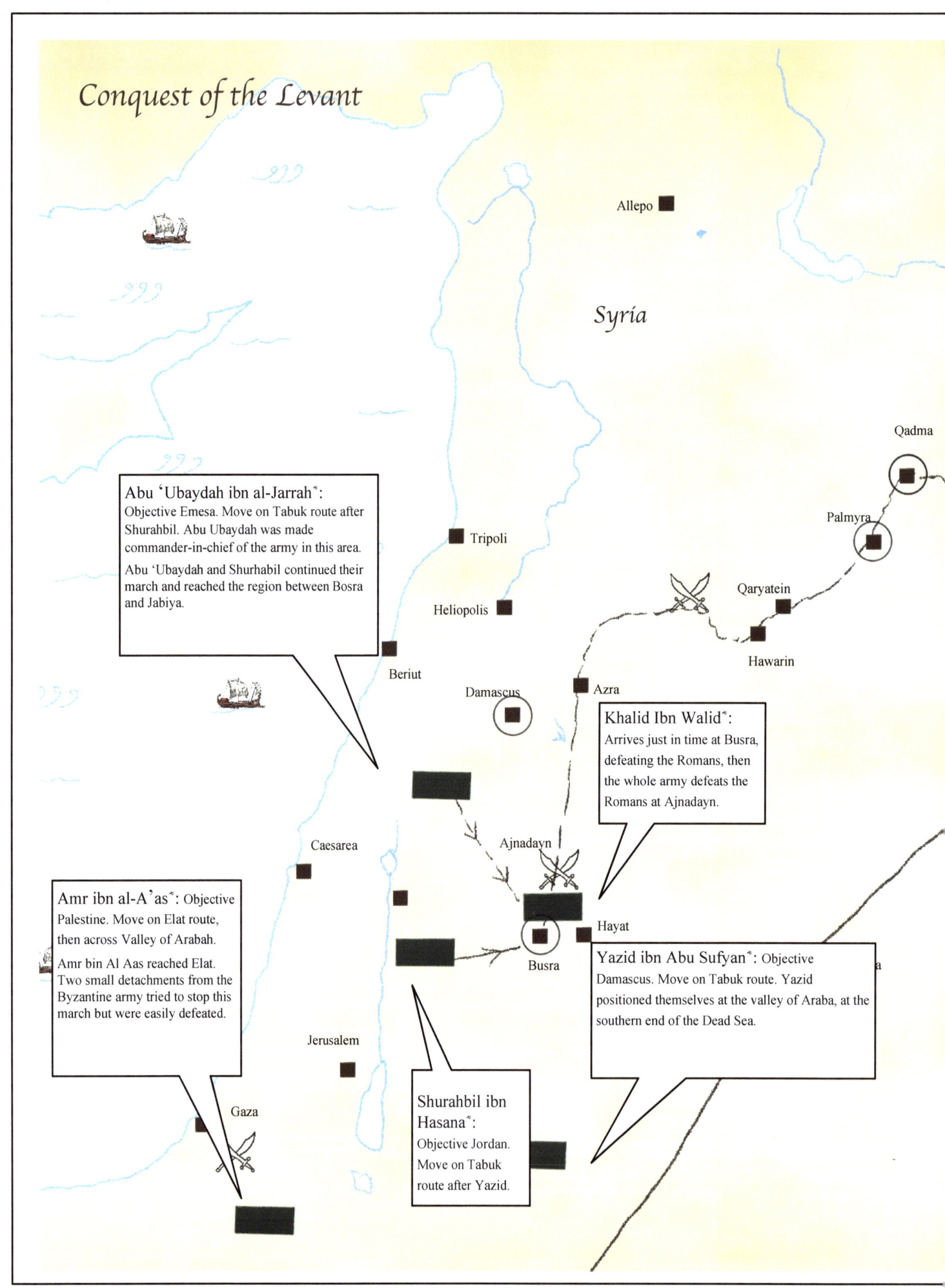

Syria

Allepo

Qadma

Palmyra

Qaryatein

Hawarin

Tripoli

Heliopolis

Beriut

Damascus

Azra

Abu 'Ubaydah ibn al-Jarrah*:
Objective Emesa. Move on Tabuk route after Shurahbil. Abu Ubaydah was made commander-in-chief of the army in this area.

Abu 'Ubaydah and Shurhabil continued their march and reached the region between Bosra and Jabiya.

Khalid Ibn Walid*:
Arrives just in time at Busra, defeating the Romans, then the whole army defeats the Romans at Ajnadayn.

Caesarea

Ajnadayn

Hayat

Amr ibn al-A'as*: Objective Palestine. Move on Elat route, then across Valley of Arabah.

Amr bin Al Aas reached Elat. Two small detachments from the Byzantine army tried to stop this march but were easily defeated.

Busra

Yazid ibn Abu Sufyan*: Objective Damascus. Move on Tabuk route. Yazid positioned themselves at the valley of Araba, at the southern end of the Dead Sea.

Jerusalem

Shurahbil ibn Hasana*: Objective Jordan. Move on Tabuk route after Yazid.

Gaza

Map

Persia

Firaz

Quradir

-------- Khalid Ibn Walid's* route

■ Muslim army

▪ City or town

◯ Siege

⚔ Major battle

|——————————————|
250 Miles

Rashidun Khulafah

THE BYZANTINES

The Byzantines made up the eastern side of the Roman Empire and were known in the time of the Prophet ﷺ simply as 'the Romans'. The Eastern Empire covered most of the Eastern Mediterranean known as the Levant - Syria, Jordan, Lebanon, Palestine, and Israel including the great cities of Jerusalem, Damascus, Antioch, Constantinople in Turkey and Alexandria in Egypt.

The Byzantines had been in conflict with the Persians for many centuries which had weakened them in manpower and resources.

The new nation of Muslims presented a potential new threat and the Byzantians bitterly remembered being defeated at the battles of Mu'tah and Tabuk during the time of the Prophet ﷺ. Still, Emperor Heraclius did not consider the Muslims as a great threat and wanted to concentrate on setting up most of his defences in northern Syria, facing the Sassanid Persians after he had re-claimed Syria.

This meant that the Muslims, who would be advancing from the desert in the south, would be able to access Byzantine lands quite easily.

Abu Bakr* split the army into four units, each with its own commander and objective. Khalid* was still in Persia when he recieved instructions for his army to immediately join the other Muslims forces.

KHALID'S* MARCH ACROSS THE DESERT

Khalid* and 10,000 men had to quickly reach Abu 'Ubayda's* army, about 500 miles away. Khalid* decided to avoid the conventional route, which was the longest, past Daumat al-Jandal, which would take weeks. Khalid* also wanted to avoid the Mesopotamian route because of the Roman soldiers positioned along it. He finally decided to pass through 300 miles of the dry Syrian desert. He spoke to locals who gave them some good advice which was to not water their thirty camels for seven days, then, once they were thirsty, allow them to drink their fill and then travel with them. Every time they camped, they had to slaughter two camels a day, water the horses, and feed the meat to the men. This worked quite well although it lasted only half of the journey and the soldiers began to get very hungry and thirsty. Fortunately, Khalid* had brought a villager along as a guide, he told them to keep travelling and at a certain point, he began to search around. He found a tree and an underground spring with enough water for everyone. The villager had only been there once before when he was a child.

Khalid ibn Walid* and his army found Abu 'Ubaydah's* army at Busra in full battle with the Romans. They were trying their best to stay alive but were overwhelmed by the Romans' numbers and battle tactics. Luckily, Khalid* arrived just at the right time, and defeated the Romans.

Story of the Battle of Ajnadayn and the Siege of Damascus

July - August 634 (13 A.H.)

As told by a fictional character, Abdul Karim.

I will never forget the look on the Romans' faces, when we surprised them a few weeks ago near Busra, as we joined Abu 'Ubaydah's army. We arrived on the ridge of a hill, after our gruelling journey on foot across the desert from Persia, and looked down to see the battle against the Romans raging in full force, the Romans had the advantage and the Muslim army was struggling.

It seemed we had arrived just in time, alhamdulillah. With battle cries, we charged down the hill. The Romans looked towards us and as they realised it was none other than Khalid ibn Walid's army, fear appeared on their faces. We engaged them forcefully and they began to lose confidence and retreated to their fort, which we then took without trouble.

After this, we travelled to Ajnadayn and met 90,000 soldiers sent by Emperor Heraclius, when I set eyes on the Roman soldiers, my heart sank. This was an enormous army, far greater than we

had been prepared for. My eyes searched for the reassuring presence of our great general, Khalid ibn Walid whose name is now renowned throughout the Roman Empire. He was extraordinary, subhaanAllah. The Prophet ﷺ named him the 'Sword of Allah' and he was unstoppable.

Across the plain, the Romans were lining up in perfect battle formations. Every soldier was equipped with identical Roman armour and large curved shields to easily protect themselves against our swords and storms of arrows. Their weapons looked solid and well-made. They stood waiting under flags of red and gold that were fluttering in the wind. To us, they looked like boys, with their pale northern skins and clean-shaven faces, although their expressions were those of experienced warriors with the confidence of having the great Byzantine Empire behind them. I caught the scent of a mixture of leather, horses, sweat and fearful defiance, their horses whinnied impatiently and shifted positions.

I looked around at the Muslim army; none of us had matching uniforms. We wore various types of helmets, turbans, some tough round or oval leather shields, and some of the finest swords in the lands. Most of us had beards, some with long black hair, and eyes rimmed with kohl that we used to protect ourselves against the desert sands. We were united in our cause and our faith.

We were ordered to tell the men to stretch our lines as far as possible so that they could not be outflanked. Of course, the Roman lines were at least four times deeper. A reserve force under Yazid Abu Sufyan* was also created for reinforcements when needed.

I finally spotted Khalid*in the distance negotiating with a Christian priest. Khalid*was undoubtedly making the three usual offers. The priest declined both the offer of Islam and of surrender to Muslim rule and so the battle commenced.

Many rounds of arrow volleys began. The Romans were able to shoot far with bigger bows and the sky was darkened with the arrows.

Now, the champions fought one to one - the Romans sent their best generals, top commanders and officers and we sent our best fighters. We won every duel.

The Romans were undoubtedly shaken by our success but this did not stop them. The battle began in earnest and we fought throughout the day. At the end of the first day, after intense fighting, we had only lost a few hundred men, but the Romans had lost thousands. The reserve force under Yazid Abu Sufyan* was used with good effect, again surprising the Romans at a key moment in the battle.

During a break in the fighting, I heard about the treacherous plan of the Romans to kill our commander, Khalid*, under a false pretence of peace. They thought they could invite Khalid*out in the open and ambush him. However, Khalid*had discovered the plot and pretended he knew nothing about it and rode out to meet the general. The general started discussing the false peace treaty when Khalid*revealed that he knew about the plan and had already dealt with the ambushers, a fight ensued and the general, although a strong fighter, was killed.

This was a major blow for the Romans. With so many officers and commanders killed, their morale was broken and they were defeated. It was a great victory for us.

After the battle, we expected to be ordered to go to Jerusalem, the main Roman city. Instead, we received orders to conquer 'the Paradise of Syria' - Damascus.

We set off and despite being delayed on the way by having to counter some Roman attacks, we arrived a few weeks later. The huge city of Damascus, surrounded by forty-five-foot stone walls, appeared before us. The turrets were high and flags were flying.

"Send the messengers in with our offer!" said Khalid ibn Walid.

Our offer was always the same: *"In the name of Allah, the Most Compassionate and Merciful. Submit to Islam and you will be free to enjoy the same rewards as the Muslims. Or, if you do not, you must agree to pay the jizya tax and in return for our protection, you will be free to practice your religions and have your own churches and synagogues. If you refuse either of these, then we let the swords decide and whoever wins, their people and property become forfeit."*

The messengers would then explain the religion of Islam to the rulers of that city.

We waited an hour or so for the messengers to return.

"Thomas, the governor of Damascus, has rejected our offer." The messenger said. Thomas was the son-in-law of Emperor Heraclius.

"Then we will let the swords decide," announced Khalid.

We all wished to do this the easy way of course, but it was not to be. The Romans would not back down easily, after all, they had been the largest empire in the world for hundreds of years.

Maybe there were as few as 15,000 soldiers inside the walls. Many of those were the wounded and exhausted remnants of the army we had just defeated. We had heard from the messengers that Heraclius, the Roman emperor, had expected us to continue to Jerusalem, so he hadn't sent any reinforcements to Damascus!

We were ordered to lay siege and position ourselves at each of the six gates. Our army at that time was about 30,000. Luckily the land was fertile, and we had found provisions. We were not allowing anything in or out of the city. Khalid had ordered all the main routes to be blocked, and the route to Medina was guarded at all times so that our supply chain was unhindered.

Around the campfire that night, as I ate the last of my dinner, I gazed over at the walls and rooftops of Damascus. The lamps of the city made the whole city seem to glow orange and yellow. I had heard stories of untold riches inside the ancient walls of Damascus. I wondered if the treasures of Damascus were as splendid as the city of Hira in Persia.

I remembered when we charged into Hira, we couldn't stop ourselves from gawping at the gold ornaments, huge buildings, and stone carvings of lions that look like people. It was all so different from my simple hometown of Medina. We'd managed to capture Hira, after a weak resistance by the Persians; something we could not even have dreamed about before the Prophet ﷺ had arrived.

I would never have imagined, even a year ago, that the Muslim lands would expand so rapidly, even though I had heard the prediction the Prophet ﷺ, made when splitting the boulder at the Battle of the Trench, with my own ears.

The men were all getting ready for 'Isha prayer so I went to do my wudu. We were in high spirits at the beginning of the siege, after so many successes. The prayers were taking place at the monastery, where Khalid, our commander, had set up the headquarters.

"Allahu Akbar… Allahu Akbar…" The adhan sounded. I hoped the inhabitants of the city could hear this beautiful call to prayer which always makes my heart swell and hope, inshAllah, the adhan would be called out from the rooftops of Damascus in the not so distant future. InshAllah we hoped this would not be a long siege considering all our recent successes.

However, we found over the next few weeks, just how high the walls of Damascus were. Our attempts at scaling them were met with showers of arrows and rocks.

Rain had made our camps soggy with mud and our tents and clothes wet. Hundreds of our tents lined the hills and plains. We were having to go further and further each day to find firewood and livestock. Alhamdulillah, we had our supply chains bringing bread and other provisions and some medical supplies for the wounded.

After the prayers and tired at the end of the day, I found my tent that I shared with my friend, Zayd. I tried to soak up some water that had seeped into the sheepskin and lay down to sleep. It seemed I had only just closed my eyes when I heard Khalid's voice command us to make ready. His voice immediately made me want to jump into action, even though I had only had one hour's sleep. I came out of the tent and saw him standing there with an air of utter determination and invincibility.

"Abdul Karim! Get the men ready. Roman reinforcements are coming so I'm sending a contingent of men to intercept them before they arrive at the city. Rafay bin Umayr is commanding."

News had arrived from scouts that an army of around 12,000 Romans were on their way.

"Yes sir!" I quickly ran from tent to tent in my designated area, keeping my voice quiet and putting out fires, unless Roman soldiers spotted our movements from the turrets of the city.

I knew we had little time before Khalid would want us to leave. He moved at speed and expected his soldiers to do the same. This is why the enemy could never keep up. It was essential that we intercepted the Romans before they reached the city.

Everyone else knew this as well and we were ready in time. About 4,000 soldiers were to stay and guard our camps, to make it look as if we were still there. The rest of us, about 16,000, marched quickly overland on the road leading to the city in the direction where Khalid knew the enemy troops were advancing.

We marched at a steady trot. The night was dark, and the trees moved eerily in the breeze. I wondered how far away the enemy was as my sandals were getting uncomfortable. I had not had a chance to replace them since I was in Medina, which seemed so long ago.

We marched on and on, with little breaks, just time for water now and then. The dawn was beginning to break on the horizon, a glimmer of blue and pink light. The early morning dew made everything glisten. As the day grew brighter, we could make out

Siege of Damascus

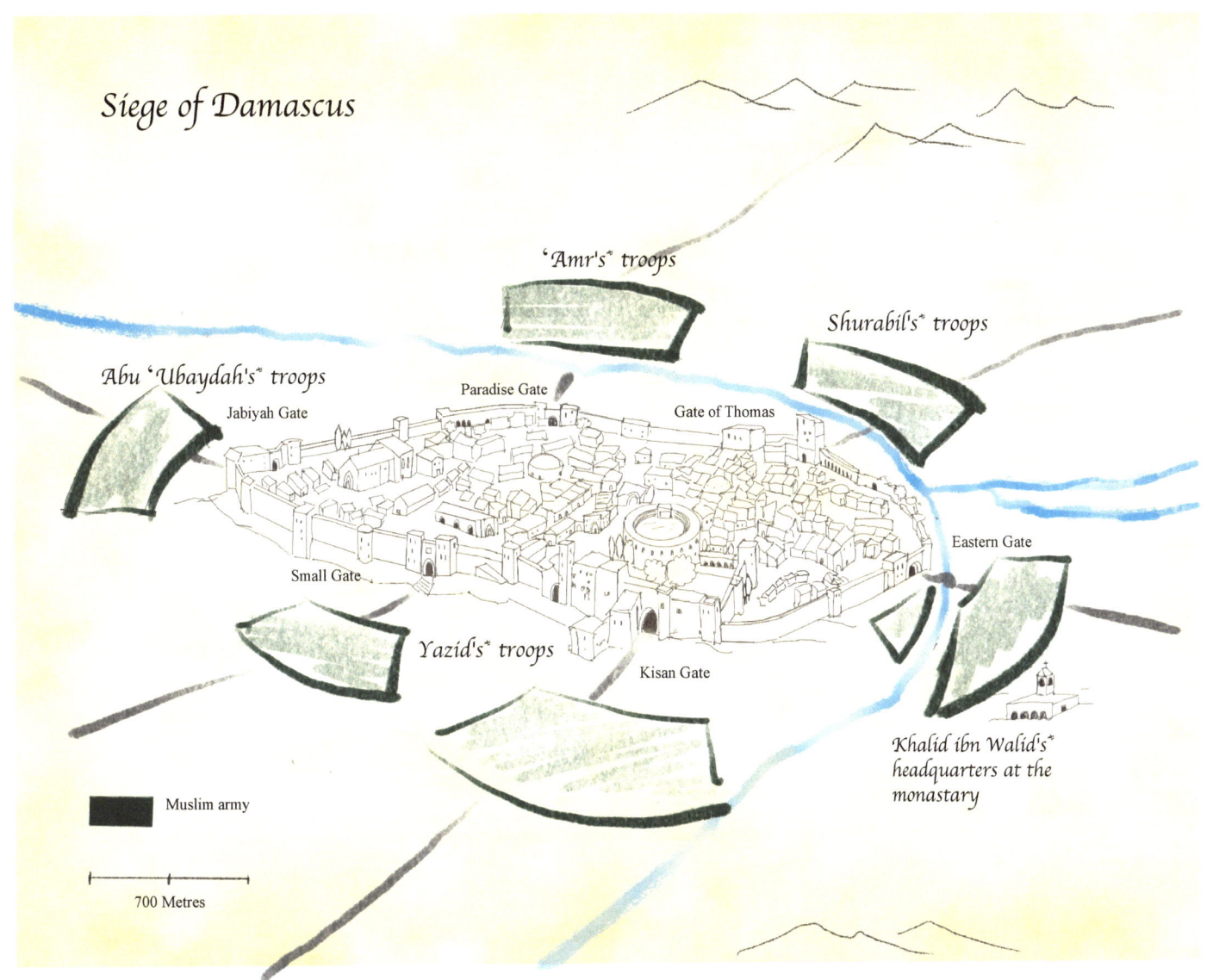

'Amr's* troops

Shurabil's* troops

Abu 'Ubaydah's* troops

Jabiyah Gate

Paradise Gate

Gate of Thomas

Small Gate

Eastern Gate

Yazid's* troops

Kisan Gate

Khalid ibn Walid's* headquarters at the monastary

Muslim army

700 Metres

our surroundings - a hilly region with some low trees, rocks and dry shrubs. The aroma of herbs filled the air. High up in the sky I could make out an eagle scanning the ground.

Suddenly we stopped and were told to be silent. The enemy had been spotted at a distance, preparing to leave their overnight campsite. It was essential they did not see us as they might change their route and reach Damascus before we could encounter them.

We dispersed behind hills that were, conveniently, on either side of the road and waited until they approached. On our commander's signal and with a shout of "Allahu Akbar!" we ran down the hill at the Roman army.

They were caught entirely off guard and we had the immediate advantage, but the Romans, having greater numbers, began to surround us. We fought hard, but I was wondering why more men had not been sent for this mission. Just then, we heard the sounds of cavalry approaching, and alhamdulillah, Khalid * himself arrived with more reinforcements! This tipped the battle decidedly in our favour, and the remaining soldiers fled after dropping their arms.

So much for the Roman reinforcements.

We then had to turn around and hurry back before the Romans at Damascus realised that much of the Muslim army was gone.

The next day, giving us no time to recover, an attack was launched at the gate of Thomas, by the governor, Thomas of Damascus. This was where Shurabil, one of the Muslim generals, was positioned with 5,000 of our men. Initially, a rain of arrows was fired down on our brothers, and then the Romans burst out of the gate with a great number of men, with Thomas leading them. Sharabil's men fought them off, but the battle was heavy. We were ordered to stay in our positions and not go to their aid unless another gate was opened.

By nightfall, both sides were exhausted and the Romans, unable to break our lines, returned inside the walls. Thomas himself was wounded in his right eye. That night another stream of Roman soldiers attacked at the Thomas gate, further weakening that side. Many of our men were wounded and some dead.

Zayd and I were sent to Abu 'Ubayda's* camp at the Jabila gate, as they needed more archers. This was on the other side of the city walls.

We arrived at his camp; Abu 'Ubayda* was one of the older companions. We had fought together at Badr, although I was only a youth then. He was very wise and a good general, but did not have the extra drive that we all saw in Khalid*. Abu 'Ubayda* would pray a lot and was very pious. It was an honour to serve him.

Abu 'Ubayda* welcomed us as we arrived. "As-salaamu 'alaykum, 'Abdul Karim and Zayd! Alhamdulillah, glad to have you with us." He smiled and directed us to the best vantage point. We joined the others and spent the next few hours fighting the Romans with no conclusion.

The next morning the Romans attacked a few gates simultaneously, including ours. They came out with fury, determination and in desperation that was created by the siege. We again fought them off, Abu 'Ubayda* commanded his troops expertly, and we forced them back into the city but we were unable to gain entry.

There was also heavy fighting at the other gates, the Small gate and the Eastern gate where Khalid* was. Our agile cavalry was brilliant at strengthening our forces where needed.

Eventually, the Romans retreated. They lost thousands of men, and they knew they could not break our ranks.

Later that night, as we finished digging the graves, we saw a group of important-looking Romans on horseback arriving at Abu 'Ubayda's tent. We reached for our weapons and went over. The Romans spoke to the guards at the entrance and were let in. I caught the guard's eye and he motioned for us to go in as well. We entered Abu 'Ubayda's tent and waited by the entrance. It was the Governor of Damascus. His beardless face was bandaged over his right eye. He was wearing fine armour over some once-white cloth, stained with blood. The Governor, Thomas, son-in-law of Emperor Heraclius, wanted to begin peace talks.

"We are weary of this siege," said Thomas, addressing Abu 'Ubayda*, "You have defeated the reinforcements that we had been waiting for and our army has not been able to break the siege. We have run out of food. Therefore, we want to accept your terms of surrender."

"Alhamdulillah, that is a good choice," said Abu 'Ubayda*. "Muslims are friends with the people of the book (The Christians and Jews) and it is never our intention to put a people in hardship. Therefore, do you agree to accept the khalifat of Abu Bakr and payment of jizya? In return, we place you under our protection...you may keep all of your belongings and are free to leave if you desire and no harm will come to you. The Christians of this city will be able to pray in peace and no harm will come to the monasteries or Churches and this applies as well to the Jewish inhabitants. You may also try yourselves under your own laws. Do you accept these terms?"

"Yes, I accept these terms." Abu 'Ubayda* and Thomas shook hands.

We then accompanied them towards the huge city gates of iron,

all eyes watching us. As we entered the city, tall buildings with detailed carved stonework towered over us on either side of the narrow streets of small paving stones. I saw many people, sitting in their doorways, the mark of hunger on their faces. They looked at us with a mixture of disbelief, fear, and curiosity. We wished that those in charge could have accepted our friendly peace treaty at the beginning, avoiding the siege and all this suffering.

We arrived at the cathedral in the centre of Damascus. Such a beautiful building. The floor was smooth marble with intricate designs; statues of Roman emperors were positioned on pillars dotted around the great hall. By Allah, I had heard of the gold of Damascus, and now seeing the glittering statues and ornaments filled my eyes with gold, I was overwhelmed and I felt my heart covet these things. I immediately looked down, remembering the simple house of the Prophet ﷺ, and begged Allah's forgiveness.

We listened and waited to see the conclusions of the treaty.

Just at that moment, we heard a great noise, and the doors to the hall crashed open. Soldiers poured into the hall, both Muslim and Roman. The Romans were struggling against the restraints of the Muslims.

Khalid ibn Walid* marched in, holding the necks of two Roman commanders shouting, "By Allah! I hereby declare we have subjugated the city of Damascus! Allahu Akbar!" He then saw 'Abu 'Ubayda* standing next to Thomas and stared incredulously, with an expression of confusion.

"We have just agreed to a peace treaty. Damascus has surrendered," Abu 'Ubayda* said.

A tense silence followed. Khalid stood there, in full battle mode, sword in his hand, his blood-stained armour glinting in the afternoon sun. Khalid had somehow managed to enter the city, probably encountering much resistance, and with great effort, fought his way to the central government chambers, where he could then claim victory. All the wealth and people of the city would then become the property of the Khalifate.

Abu 'Ubayda* and Khalid ibn Walid*, stared at one another. They then moved to the side of the room to discuss the matter.

"Muslims do not go back on their word, once an agreement is in place," Abu 'Ubayda* said.

Khalid* replied, "But Thomas most likely knew that I had attacked, that is why he rushed to your camp to ask for surrender - therefore the city was taken before it had surrendered!" Abu 'Ubayda paused to contemplate what the Holy Prophet ﷺ would advise.

At the other end of the room, Thomas, who knew of Khalid's warlike nature, looked tensely back and forth between the two, unsure if to say anything.

Little had the camp of Abu 'Ubayda* realised, but yesterday night, a man from Damascus, whom they called Jonah 'the lover', sneaked out of the city. He was especially tired of the siege because he wanted to marry his fiance and the siege was getting in the way. Jonah informed them that there was to be a festival the next day, and almost everyone, including the soldiers, would be drinking and enjoying the festival.

This was the break that Khalid ibn Walid had been praying for. With the soldiers drunk, they could scale the walls and enter the city relatively unhindered. News of this plan, by Allah's decree, had not reached our camp, hence the confusion.

Khalid and Abu 'Ubayda spoke between themselves.

"Very well, we accept your surrender because 'Ubaydallah has given his word!" Khalid announced.

Thomas let out a sigh of relief.

There were celebrations that night. Now that the siege was over, Damascus was officially part of the ever-growing Muslim lands, alhumdulillah. May it continue to prosper.

Part of the agreement was that the Roman army was to leave the city immediately, otherwise, the Muslim army could re-engage them in battle in three days' time.

Khalid wrote this letter to the people of Damascus:

"In the name of Allah, the Beneficent, the Merciful. This is given by Khalid bin al-Waleed to the people of Damascus. When the Muslims enter, they (the people) shall have safety for themselves, their property, their temples and the walls of their city, of which nothing shall be destroyed. They have this guarantee on behalf of Allah, the Messenger of Allah, the Khalifa and the Muslims, from whom they shall receive nothing but good so long as they pay the jizya."

During the siege, I had heard of the passing of Abu Bakr and my heart was still heavy with sorrow. Now that the siege was over, I longed to get back to Medina, to my wife and child. It seemed like an eternity since I had walked the peaceful streets of Medina and prayed in the Prophet's ﷺ Mosque.

19th century lithograph of the Damascus Gate, Jerusalem

Abu Bakr's Passing to the Next Life

On 23 August 634 (13 A.H.), while the armies were still in Syria, Abu Bakr fell sick. He developed a high fever and was confined to bed. His illness was prolonged, and when his condition worsened, he felt that his end was near. He asked his daughter 'Aisha before he died, "On what day did the Prophet die ?"

She replied, "He died on a Monday."

And he asked, "And how was he buried?"

She answered, "He was buried with three white garments, without any turban." Abu Bakr was wearing a white garment at the time but it had a small stain, so he asked Aisha to wash off the stain. He then requested two more white garments and asked Sayyidina 'Ali to perform his ghusl or funeral wash when the time came.

Before he passed to the next life, Abu Bakr wanted to nominate his successor so that there would not be any doubts about who was to be the next khalifah after his death. He appointed 'Umar to be the next Khalifa after discussing the matter with some Companions, some of whom were not sure because of the tough nature of 'Umar. However, Abu Bakr felt sure of his decision.

Abu Bakr thus dictated his last testament to 'Uthman ibn Affan as follows:

"In the name of the Most Merciful God. This is the last will and testament of Abu Bakr bin Abu Quhafa, when he is in the last hour of the world, and the first of the next; an hour in which the infidel must believe, the wicked be convinced of their evil ways, I nominate 'Umar bin al-Khattab as my successor. Therefore, heed him and obey him. If he acts right, confirm his actions. My intentions are good, but I cannot see the future results. However, those who do ill shall render themselves liable to severe account hereafter. Fare you well. May you be ever attended by the Divine Favour of blessing."

Abu Bakr's illness grew worse and he returned to God on a Monday, as did the Prophet, between the evening and night prayers on the 22nd of Jumada al-Akhir, 634 (13 A.H.). The Holy Prophet once said to him, "Abu Bakr, you will be the first of my people to enter Paradise."

He was then washed and buried beside the Prophet in Aisha's house. He remains there to this day, in the Masjid an-Nabawi in Medina.

Calligraphy that says Abu Bakr as-Siddique

ABU BAKR'S LIFE IN THE LIGHT OF JIHAD

Abu Bakr spent his life in Jihad, following the perfect example set by the Holy Prophet.

During his khalifate, Abu Bakr was forced to engage in Jihad of the Sword, due to the many rebellions and threats from other Empires. In this, he sought guidance from the Prophet and was successful in all his endeavours.

He also continued the Prophet's Jihad of Education, teaching everything that he had learnt from the Prophet, ensuring that the Prophet's teachings were preserved. Through him, the religion of Islam was supported and protected.

In the Jihad of the Hand, he fought hard to ensure that the social justice and welfare established by the Prophet continued. There are always so many people who thrive on oppression who would have benefited if things had returned to how they were, but Abu Bakr prevented that from happening. He was the only khalifah in the history of Islam who refunded to the State Treasury, at the time of his death, the entire amount of the allowance that he had drawn during the period of his khalifah.

Spiritually, or in the Jihad of the Heart, he was the mirror of the Prophet, maintaining a very pious life, he was a fountain of knowledge for the Believers and their spiritual leader. He said, "Whoever fights his ego (*nafs*) for the sake of Allah, He will protect him against what he dislikes."

May Allah bless him and grant him peace - *Ameen.*

Chromolithograph by an Indian artist 1900. Abu Bakr as-Siddique is buried in the Masjid an Nawabi, Medina, Saudi Arabia, next to his best friend, the Prophet Muhammadﷺ.

Famous Quotes of Abu Bakr as-Siddique

"He should know that his heart is empty of faith when good advice has no effect on him."

"Run away from greatness and greatness will follow you."

"Good actions are a guard against the blows of adversity."

"Without knowledge action is useless and knowledge without action is futile."

A prayer: "O Allah, make me better than what they think of me, and forgive me what they do not know of me and do not take me to account for what they say about me."

"The more knowledge you have, the greater your fear of Allah will be."

Allah hu Haqq by Hana Horack-Elyafi

35

Profile - Khalid ibn Walid

The Prophet ﷺ said, "Khalid is truly an excellent slave of Allah and a brother of the same tribe. He is a sword of Allah unsheathed against disbelievers and hypocrites."

Khalid ibn Walid is undoubtedly the most famous and celebrated warrior in Islamic history and considered one of the top three military leaders of all time, if not the best. He was a military genius, extremely brave, and absolutely determined. He was incredibly successful and an undefeated general. He fought and commanded over two hundred battles and won every single one.

It was not just Arabian tribesmen he was successful against but also the huge and very powerful armies of the Romans and the Persians; against far greater numbers of better armed and well-trained soldiers. According to some accounts, he won the battle at Basra against the Romans just by turning up!

"Submit to Islam and be safe. Or agree to the payment of the Jizya (tax), and you and your people will be under our protection, else you will have only yourself to blame for the consequences, for I bring the men who desire death as ardently as you desire life." Khalid's invitation to leaders and generals.

HIS EARLY LIFE

Khalid grew up in one of the most wealthy clans in Makkah with his four brothers. His father was so wealthy that he alone bought the cloth for the Kaaba one year, and everyone else in Makkah pooled their money to buy it the next year.

Khalid was known for his strength and wrestling ability and was soon one of the best warriors in Makkah. He was tall and broad-shouldered, similar to Sayyidina 'Umar in looks.

In his youth, Khalid was against the Prophet ﷺ and his mission, seeing him as a rival to his family's high position in Makkah so he joined in the persecution of the Muslims; fighting against them in the battle of 'Uhud.

When the Muslims and the Quraysh were signing the treaty of Hudaybiyyah, Khalid decided it would be a good time to attack and came out with 200 men against the Muslims. He planned to wait until they were all praying and in sajda, with their heads to the ground, so they couldn't see him approaching. However, Allah had revealed the special prayer for wartime to the Prophet ﷺ: one group is standing, while another is bowing. Khalid then said, "This man is someone we will not be able to harm. I cannot even get close to him. This man is going to lead and this man is going to be victorious."

Khalid's brother, al-Walid ibn Walid, was taken captive by the Muslims and ransomed for a high price. One of his brothers went to Medina to free al-Walid and paid the ransom. When they returned to Makkah, al-Walid announced he was a Muslim. They asked him why he decided not to declare his Islam back in Medina and to be free? Walid said that he wanted to accept Islam as a free man so that no one could say he did it out of fear or to save money. Al-Walid then went back to Medina and became a close Companion of the Prophet ﷺ.

KHALID'S CONVERSION TO ISLAM

A little while later, Khalid received a letter from him: "You are an intelligent man, can you not see the truth of Islam? The Prophet ﷺ has been asking about you. He asks 'Where is Khalid? Allah will bring him along.'"

Khalid then saw a dream. He narrates, "I saw myself on a piece of land that was dry and very narrow. Then I saw myself travelling to a beautiful green piece of land that was very broad." He decided to go to Medina.

He went to speak to his friends and found two of them, 'Uthman ibn Talha and 'Amr ibn 'Aas, who also wanted to accept Islam. In great happiness, they went together to Medina and were met by Walid ibn Walid, who came rushing over and said, "The Prophet ﷺ has already informed us that you will be coming over!"

"As-salaamu 'alaykum yaa Rasoolullah," Khalid said as he entered the room.

"Wa 'alaykum as-salaam Khalid" replied the Prophet ﷺ. "Look at this, the Quraysh has thrown out its liver!" By this, the Prophet ﷺ meant the strongest part.

Khalid said, "But I caused so much harm against Islam, what will happen to me? Please forgive me!"

"I can inform you that coming to Islam wipes out all previous sins," replied the Prophet ﷺ kindly. Khalid asked to hear this three times from the Prophet ﷺ. Then Khalid ibn Walid, the greatest warrior of the Quraysh, said his shahada.

An illustration by Marwan Musa of what Khalid ibn Walid ؓ may have looked like.

KHALID'S ؓ MILITARY CAREER

He rose quickly in the ranks of the Muslim army. In only a matter of months, at the battle of Mu'ta, when the fighting of the Byzantines was intense and the standard passed three times, Khalid ibn Walid ؓ was handed the standard. Khalid ؓ humbly accepted and changed the course of the battle, saving hundreds of lives.

Although he did not feel he was worthy, Khalid ibn Walid ؓ had the great honour of entering Makkah for the final conquest, positioned to the left of the Prophet ﷺ.

After the Prophet ﷺ died, such was his love for the Prophet Muhammad ﷺ, he always carried a hair of the Holy Prophet ﷺ in his helmet. When he lost his helmet in the battle of Yarmuk, he exhausted himself and others hunting for it. When he was criticised for that, he said, "I keep it for luck, for it has some hairs of the Prophet ﷺ. It makes me feel optimistic that victory is within reach."

Khalid ibn Walid ؓ is the most celebrated commander in Islam. Undefeated, he acted with nobility and justice, caring not for his own position and power.

In battle, he was never cruel and followed the way of the Prophet ﷺ. He was a fierce fighter, and very good at gathering intelligence.

Khalid ibn Walid* was absolutely determined on the battlefield and acted quickly and decisively, before the enemy had time to think, out-manoeuvring the enemy on every occasion. He did not allow his army to sleep when action needed to be taken.

He was excellent at gathering intelligence, sending spies and scouts further ahead to find out what the enemy's plans were and to understand the lay of the land. Often commanders and soldiers from the opposing army would join the Muslims and give essential information.

He operated under the Islamic Code of Conduct established by the Prophet Muhammad ﷺ which forbade the killing of women and children, livestock, and crops and enjoined good treatment of the captured (no torture). Some Byzantine emperors would practise horrific punishments and have their enemies' heads served on a platter, a terrible common practice. Unfortunately, this practice became popular with some later Islamic Dynasties.

When a city surrendered and agreed to pay the jizya (non-Muslim tax), Khalid* would order the Muslim army to immediately stop all fighting. They would also return all the captured people.

His enemies could appeal to his justice and receive an honest response. When Emperor Heraclius asked for the return of his daughter who had been captured after the siege of Damascus, Khalid* sent her to her father, asking for no ransom.

Khalid* said that it was faith that drove him.

Emperor Heraclius observed,

"The army prays regularly and cares not for this world."

A Christian priest warned of Khalid's* army.

"Is the standard of this army a black one? Is the commander of this army a tall, powerfully built, broad-shouldered man with a large beard and a few pock marks on his face? Then beware of fighting this army."

STORY OF A ROMAN SOLDIER

Once, a Roman officer, Jerjah, asked to see Khalid* during a break in the fighting. He had been very impressed by Khalid.* When they met, the commander asked him, "Khalid tell me the truth, for a freedman does not lie. Did God send down on your Prophet a heavenly sword that he gave to you so that it enables you to kill anyone that comes within its sweep?"

Khalid answered, "No."

"Then why do they call you the Sword of Allah?"

Khalid* explained, "Allah sent His Prophet to us. Some of us believed him and others disbelieved in him. I was among the disbelievers until Allah guided my heart to Islam and to His Prophet ﷺ and I gave him my allegiance. Then the Prophet ﷺ prayed for me and said, 'You are the Sword of Allah.'"

The Roman said, "So what do you invite people to?"

"We invite people to monotheism and to Islam."

He asked, "Does anyone who submits himself to Islam have the same reward as you?" Khalid* answered, "Yes, and even better."

"How is that?"

"We lived with the Prophet ﷺ and saw with our own eyes his signs and miracles, anyone who saw and heard what we saw and heard was expected to submit to Islam sooner or later. As for you who did not see or hear him, if despite this, you believe in him and in the unseen, you will find better and greater reward if you purify your conscience and intentions to Allah."

The Roman commander then took his shahada and fought on the Muslim side until he gained martyrdom.

Relief of the Arabian goddesses Al-Lat, Manat, and al-'Uzza

Tomb of Khalid ibn Walid in Syria before it was destroyed in 2018 by Bashar Assad forces.

AL-'UZZA

Shortly after the Conquest of Makkah, Muhammad ﷺ began efforts to eliminate the last cult images reminiscent of pre-Islamic practices. Al-'Uzza had been considered the most important goddess in the region.

He sent Khalid ibn Walid during Ramadan 630 AD (8 AH) to a place called Nakhlah, where the goddess al-'Uzza was worshipped by the tribes of Quraysh and Kinanah. The shrine's custodians were from Banu Shayban.

The Prophet ﷺ ordered Khālid ibn Walid to destroy what people thought of as al-'Uzza, who was supposed to inhabit one of three trees. (Sometimes a jinn can be confused with a god and can inhabit trees and other objects.)

Ibn al-Kalbi relates:

"Khalid destroyed the first one and returned to Muhammad to report. Muhammad replied, asking whether something eventful happened, which Khalid denied. The same thing happened after cutting down the second tree. When Khalid was about to destroy the last tree, a woman with wild hair appeared. Al-Sulami, the custodian of al-'Uzza, was there and gave the order to kill Khalid. Khalid struck the woman down with his sword and chopped her head off at which she fell down in a pile of ashes. Khalid went on to kill Sulami and cut the last tree. When he returned to Muhammad, Muhammad is recounted to have said that the woman was al-'Uzza, and she shall never be worshipped again."

HIS PASSING TO THE NEXT LIFE

Khalid fiercely wanted to attain the rank of martyrdom but this was not to be his destiny.

He said to Sayyidina 'Umar when lying on his deathbed, "All the battles I fought have left my body scarred with wounds and stabs everywhere, yet here I am dying in bed as if I have never witnessed war before."

Sayyidina 'Umar replied, "It is not fitting that the 'Sword of Allah' is killed by an unbeliever." With that, Khalid's heart was at rest.

He also said on his deathbed, "I was busy on the battlefield and couldn't learn much about the Qur'an. But I have no regrets. I have served Allah."

Sayyidina 'Umar cried excessively upon his death. This was not only because of a great loss to the nation of Islam but also that 'Umar did not get a chance to return him to his post, as he had intended, now that the people were less infatuated with him.

Khalid ibn Walid cared not for the riches that he could have amassed on his conquests. Instead, when he died, he gave 'Umar his most treasured possessions: his horse and his weapons.

His mother recited these lines of poetry as his body was carried to the grave, "Do you ask me about his valour? He was more courageous than a huge lion that protects its cubs in times of danger. Do you ask me about his generosity? He was far more generous than an overwhelming torrential rain that slides down from the mountains."

Sayyidina 'Umar said, as he was buried, "May Allah have mercy on you, Abu Sulayman. What you have now is far better than what you had in life, for you are now with Allah. You were honoured in life and content with death."

Khalid ibn Walid was buried in Homs, Syria in 642 (21 A.H.).

May Allah bless Khalid ibn Walid - ameen.

Sayyidina 'Umar ibn Al-Khattab

Sayyidina 'Umar is one of the greatest Companions of the Prophet ﷺ. His love for the Prophet ﷺ and of Islam was paramount. He was an expert jurist well known for his pious and just nature which earned him the title 'Al-Faruq' which means 'the one who distinguishes (between right and wrong).' He would go to great lengths to protect the rights of all people, as we will soon hear.

He was one of the first forty people to accept Islam and one of the ten men who were promised Paradise with no account. 539 hadiths or traditions came from him. The Prophet ﷺ highlighted many times how righteous and truthful 'Umar was. His companions said, "It seemed as if the wisdom of mankind was hidden in the heart of Sayyidina 'Umar." Many of his judgments would, later on, be revealed in the Qur'an.

Prophet Muhammad ﷺ said, "If there were to be a prophet after me, it would be 'Umar, the son of al-Khattab." (Ahmad, at-Tirmidhi, Hakim)

The Prophet ﷺ said, "O son of al-Khattab, in Whose Hands is my life, if the devil sees you coming down one road, he quickly crosses the road and goes down another." (Saad ibn Abi Waqqa, Bukhari)

Ibn A'sikar narrates, "We used to say that the devils were chained up during the rule of 'Umar, and were unleashed when he perished."

The Prophet ﷺ said, "Truly Allah placed truth upon the tongue of 'Umar, the son of Khattab, and upon his heart." (Darulsalaam)

"He was full of resolution and vigilance, and wisdom and dignity." 'Ali Ibn Al-Talib

'Umar's Early Life

Sayyidina 'Umar, may Allah be well pleased with him, was born in Makkah to the Banu Adi clan. The Banu Adi clan would often settle arguments between the tribes and so they were known for peacemaking and diplomacy as well as public speaking.

His father, Khattab ibn Nufayl, was a merchant and was famed for his intelligence among his tribe. His mother was Hantama bint Hisham, from the tribe of Banu Makhzum.

In his youth, he used to tend to his father's camels in the plains near Makkah. 'Umar said, "My father, al-Khattab was a ruthless man. He used to make me work hard; if I didn't work he used to beat me and he used to work me to exhaustion."

'Umar learned how to read and write and used to love poetry and literature. He also enjoyed martial arts, horse riding, and wrestling. Because he was tall and physically powerful, he became a renowned wrestler.

Later, 'Umar decided to become a merchant and made several journeys to Rome and Persia, where he is said to have met various scholars and was interested in Roman and Persian societies. He wasn't a very successful merchant however and did enjoy drinking, as many Arabs did in the pre-Islamic days.

'Umar became one of the chiefs of the Quraysh and had the role of an envoy, or a representative, who used to negotiate with other tribes.

He is described as being very tall with a large build. His skin was pale with a slightly ruddy complexion and he had a large moustache with tinges of red at the ends.

'UMAR'S CONVERSION

In his youth, 'Umar was one of the people who were very much against Islam. Both he and Abu Jahl were prominent leaders of the Quraysh who had a lot of power and influence and would persecute the Muslims. 'Umar however was primarily against Islam because it was dividing the people of Makkah and causing problems, rather than the message. He was one of the leaders and so wanted Makkah to be a peaceful place.

One night Prophet Muhammad ﷺ prayed that Allah guides either Abu Jahl or 'Umar ibn al-Khattab to Islam.

The next day, 'Umar finally decided that he was going to slay this new 'troublemaker', the Prophet of Islam ﷺ, who was preaching in a way that went against their tribal values, thus upsetting a lot of people. 'Umar grabbed his sword and headed

off to where he thought the Prophet ﷺ was. On his way, he met Nu'aym bin 'Abdullah, who had secretly converted to Islam.

"Where are you going 'Umar?" Nu'aym asked.

'Umar told him that he was going to kill Muhammad ﷺ.

"By God, you have deceived yourself, O 'Umar! Do you think that Banu Abd Manaf would let you run around alive once you had killed their son Muhammad? Why don't you return to your own house and at least set it straight?" Nu'aym suggested going and seeing his sister first and her husband, Sa'id ibn Zayd, who had both converted to Islam.

'Umar was startled by these words. "What?" he thought to himself, "My own sister embracing Islam?!" Now even more furious he stormed over to her house and entered, demanding to know if they had accepted Islam. He heard them from outside the door reciting a surah from the Qur'an. 'Umar barged in and began quarrelling with Sa'id and his sister stepped in between. 'Umar then slapped his sister and she fell to the ground, her cheek bleeding. This shocked 'Umar who stopped.

"O enemy of God!" 'Umar's sister cried, "Suppose the truth were in another religion than yours?! I bear witness that there is no God but God and that Muhammad is His messenger!"

Something in 'Umar changed and he wanted to see the parchment that the verses were written. They asked him to perform ablution first, which he did, and then he listened to these words of the Qur'an:

"We have not sent down the Qur'an unto you (O Muhammad) to cause you distress, but only as a reminder to those who fear God. A revelation from Him who has created the Earth and high Heavens. The Most Beneficent rose over the Mighty Throne (in a manner that suits His Majesty). To Him belongs all that is in the Heavens and all that is on the Earth, and all that is between them, and all that is under the soil. And if you, O Muhammad, speak aloud, then verily, He knows the secret and that which is yet more hidden. No one has the right to be worshipped but He! To Him belong the Best Names." (20:2-8)

He asked to be taken to see the Prophet ﷺ, at the house where he was hidden. When they first saw him, the Muslims, including Hamza, who had only converted three days before, were unsure of his intentions, but 'Umar soon announced his new faith and the cries of, "Allahu Akbar!" was heard in Makkah and as far as the Heavens where the angels were also joining in at 'Umar's proclamation of faith. They knew what a man he was to become.

'Umar saw no reason why they should not be able to pray in the open at the Ka'aba, and they strode forth and began their prayers and were not disturbed because of the status of 'Umar in Makkah as a tribal chief. The Muslims could now come out into the open.

THE MUSLIMS CAN PRAY OPENLY

'Abdullah bin Mas'oud said, "'Umar's embracing Islam was our victory, his migration to Medina was our success, and his reign a blessing from Allah. We didn't offer prayers in Al-Haram Mosque until Umar had accepted Islam. When he accepted Islam, the Quraysh were compelled to let us pray (at the Ka'aba)."

'Umar wanted to proclaim his Islam openly and made a public announcement. The people were furious and began to beat him until his uncle said, "I give my protection to my sister's son." They stopped beating him but 'Umar, whose love of justice was already strong, did not like the fact he had a special privilege because of his powerful family while the other Muslims were being persecuted. He gave up the protection of his uncle. 'Umar said, "I did not stop from beating and being beaten until the establishment of Islam."

'Umar migrated to Medina soon after the Prophet ﷺ and stayed in Muhammad ibn Maslamah's house, one of the Ansar (helpers) of Medina.

'Umar took part in all the battles and being an excellent fighter, was a key figure in the time of the Prophet ﷺ, and in the Ridda wars.

'Umar was known for his strictness, unquestioning loyalty and a defender of the Prophet ﷺ.

When Abu Bakr appointed him as Khalifa, some of the high-ranking advisers were concerned that 'Umar would be too strict. To them, Abu Bakr replied: "His ('Umar's) strictness was there because of my softness. When the weight of the Khalifa will be over his shoulders, he will no longer be strict. If I will be asked by God to whom I have appointed my successor, I will tell him that I have appointed the best man among your men."

Abu Bakr As-Siddique nominated 'Umar to succeed him which was met with unanimous approval from the other Companions and 'Umar became Khalifa in the year 634 (13AH).

Sayyidina 'Umar as Khalif

Sayyidina 'Umar worried about the wealth flooding into Medina from the Northern territories of Syria and Persia. There was so much money he did not know what to do with it. He decided to give away all of it before the end of the year. He gave even more to the poor and decided to make a professional army, with every soldier being paid a yearly allowance. He gave away money to nobles in Persia and Syria who had lost property and wealth. 'Umar also gave to the remaining wives of the Prophet ﷺ.

Sayyidina 'Umar led a very humble and simple life, like that of the Prophet ﷺ, and kept no wealth for himself, only allowing him and his family enough to live on. They lived in a simple mud hut, and he often wore worn-out shoes and was usually clad in patched-up garments.

"Truly nothing is lawful to 'Umar of what belongeth to the Lord, except two garments, a garment for winter and one for summer, and what may enable him to perform the pilgrimage and the religious visitations, and my sustenance and that of my family is like a man of the Quraysh, neither the richest nor the poorest of them. Beyond this, I am but a man of the Muslims."

A busy Muslim town

NEW GOVERNORS

There were now lots of positions within the Islamic territories, from Damascus to Egypt. When 'Umar appointed someone, his orders would include:

- Do not ride in fancy carriages

- Avoid eating delicacies

- Do not wear fancy clothes

- Do not close the doors against the needy

Limitations on wealth were also set for governors and officials, who would often be dismissed if they showed any outward signs of pride or wealth which might distinguish them from the people.

'Umar wished to remove class differences so people would have the same opportunities. 'Umar also made sure that the public treasury was not wasted on unnecessary luxuries as he believed that the money would be better spent if it went towards the welfare of the people.

Even Khalid ibn Walid was summoned when 'Umar learned that he had paid a sum to a poet for writing a poem about the great Khalid ibn Walid.

He said the way he governed was simple: "I frequently change their rulers."

KINDNESS AND COMPASSION

Sayyidina 'Umar was especially concerned with the affairs of the people and would roam the streets in the evening to enquire about everyone's welfare and see if he could find some injustice that had occurred.

One night, the Amir al-Mu'mineen (Prince of the Faithful), as he came to be known, was wandering the streets to see if there were any in need and he overheard a woman lamenting about how much she missed her husband as he was away with the army. 'Umar then made a law that soldiers should not be away from their homes for more than four months.

One day, the Companion, Talha was following 'Umar and saw him go into a simple house. He was curious about this and the following day he went to the house. He knocked on the door and an old blind woman answered. Talha asked her about the man who came the day before. She said, "He comes every so often to clean my house and bring me some food." The old lady did not know who it was. "Subhaan-Allah," said Talha, "This is the Prince of the Faithful that cleans your house!"

GREAT FAMINE IN 638 (17 A.H.)

In 638 CE, Arabia fell into severe drought followed by famine. Soon after, the reserves of food in Medina began to run out. Everyone was starving, including the Khalifah, who would say to his stomach, "You may growl or not growl, but you will not taste meat until the children of Medina are fed." 'Umar ordered caravans of supplies from Syria and Iraq and personally supervised their distribution. Abu 'Ubaydah ibn al-Jarrah, the governor of Syria and the supreme commander of the army was the first to send supplies. 'Umar's order saved countless lives throughout Arabia.

Later, Abu 'Ubaydah came to Medina and was put in charge of food distribution. Sayyidina 'Umar hosted a dinner every night at Medina, which according to one estimate, had an attendance of more than a hundred thousand people.

'Umar also introduced food rationing using coupons, which were given to those in need and could be exchanged for wheat and flour.

HUMILITY AND PIETY

He would admonish himself, "Fear Allah or He will punish you." One day, when he felt himself important, he went to the mosque and up the minbar. After praising Allah, he said, "I used to be a shepherd and was paid a few handfuls of dates."

His ring said, "Death is a sufficient admonisher," this means the knowledge that you are going to die one day and the punishment of the grave will be enough to keep you doing good actions and not be proud.

Ibn Kathir said that "'Umar would pray Isha with the people then enter his house and not cease praying until dawn, and he did not die before aquiring the habit of fasting permanantly."

He sent an urgent massage to his deputies and governors:

"Your most important and urgent matter, in my view, is prayer. Whoever guards it well and persistantly has guarded his religion and whoever is careless with it is even more careless with everything else."

GREAT PLAGUE OF AMWAS

While the famine was ending in Arabia, many districts in Syria and Palestine were devastated by Bubonic plague. While 'Umar was on his way to visit Syria, he was received by Abu 'Ubaydah ibn al-Jarrah, the governor of Syria, who informed him about the plague and its intensity, and suggested that 'Umar go back to Medina. 'Umar tried to persuade Abu 'Ubaydah to come with him to Medina, but he did not want to leave his troops in that difficult situation. Unfortunately, Abu 'Ubaydah caught the plague and died, which also cost the lives of 25,000 Muslims including many Companions of the Prophet ﷺ. After the plague had weakened, in late 639, 'Umar visited Syria to reorganise government positions as most of the veteran commanders and governors had died of the plague. According to Hadith, those who die from the plague are to be considered martyrs.

Supporting the Ummah

During his khalifa and after consulting with the poor, 'Umar further developed support for the poor, widows, orphans and pensioners.

BENEFIT PAYMENTS/SOCIAL SECURITY

This was made for those people who were injured or had lost their ability to work. It became the state's responsibility to make sure that their minimum needs were met, with the unemployed and their families receiving an allowance from the public treasury. However, in order to avoid some citizens taking advantage of government services, begging and laziness were not tolerated and those who received government benefits were expected to be active members of the community.

POVERTY THRESHOLD

Another innovative concept that was introduced was that of a poverty threshold, with efforts made to ensure a minimum standard of living, making sure that no citizen across the empire would suffer from hunger. To determine the poverty line, 'Umar ordered an experiment to test how many seers of flour would be required to feed a person for a month. He found that 25 seers of flour could feed 30 people, so he concluded that 50 seers of flour would be sufficient to feed a person for a month. As a result, he ordered that the poor each receive a food ration of fifty seers of flour per month. In addition, the poor and disabled were guaranteed cash stipends.

RETIREMENT PENSIONS

These were provided to elderly people who could count on receiving a stipend (payment) from the public treasury.

ORPHAN FUND

Abandoned babies were taken care of, with one hundred dirhams spent annually on each orphan's development. 'Umar also introduced the concept of a charitable trust. For example, he bought land from the Banu Harithah and converted it into a charitable trust, which meant that profit and produce from the land went towards benefiting the poor, slaves, and travellers.

Franz Xaver - Merchants in Arab Market 19th century

Camels with Howdah by Adolphe Rouargue 1855

FREE TRADE

As new countries joined the Islamic community, they benefited from free trade throughout the lands. 'Umar established a tax for imported goods for those foreign traders who wanted to trade with the Muslims. However things like foods or cheaper products were not taxed. 'Umar also made the first coins in Islam and regulated the coins to be fair and standardised across the lands.

CANALS

Since Medina, with a rapidly growing population and with semi-desert conditions was at risk of famines, 'Umar decided to import grain when crops failed.

He ordered the building of a canal connecting the Nile to the Red Sea and improved the port on the Arabian coast. When the new city of Basra was being established during 'Umar's rule, he ordered the building of a nine-mile canal from the Tigris to the city for irrigation and drinking water. Al-Tabari reports that 'Utba ibn Ghazwan built the first part of the canal from the Tigris River to the site of Basra when the city was in the planning stage. After the city was built, 'Umar appointed Abu Musa Ashaari as its first governor. He then began to build two more important canals, the al-Ubulla and the Ma'qil, linking Basra with the Tigris River.

These two canals brought much agricultural development to the whole Basra region and were also used for drinking water. 'Umar also adopted a policy of assigning barren lands to farmers and helped them build irrigations canal, making the land fertile. This policy continued during the Umayyad period.

INFRASTRUCTURE

He was also the first to formally organise provinces, cities and districts, each with it's own local governor. He also established guest houses on all the major routes between cities.

OTHER IMPROVEMENTS FOR THE 'UMMA

Al-Askari says 'Umar was the first person who used the Hijri calendar, gathered the people in Tarawih prayers, and introduced four takbirs during the funeral prayers. In addition, anyone who memorised the entire Qur'an received a stipend. 'Umar is regarded by Sunni Muslims as one of the greatest Faqaha, and, as such, he started the process of codifying Islamic Law, known as Fiqh or Islamic Jurisprudence.

He used to ensure the Mosques were lit with lamps so that 'Ali ibn Talib said, "May the Lord illuminate 'Umar in his grave as he has illuminated our Mosques." (Ibn Asakir, Isma-b-Ziyad)

In 17 A.H., 'Umar enlarged the Prophet's Mosque and placed small pebbles on the ground.

'Umar suggested that it would be good to have a new calendar, marking the advent of Islam. There was some debate as to when it should begin - when the Prophet ﷺ was born or when he died? 'Ali suggested it should be when the Prophet ﷺ migrated to Medina and with that, everyone agreed.

He refused to chop off the hands of thieves because he felt their thievery was a result of his falling short of his responsibility to provide meaningful employment to all his subjects. As a ruler of a vast kingdom, his vision was to ensure that everyone in his kingdom should sleep on a full stomach. He didn't only have a vision; he truly transformed his vision into actions.

Canals were used to bring water to much needed dry land so that it could be farmed.

On the Battle Front

During the Khilafah of 'Umar[ra], times were noticeably peaceful among the Muslims, with few rebellions, unlike the Khilafah of Abu Bakr, 'Uthman and 'Ali. The Prophet ﷺ described him as, "A firmly bolted door between the Muslims and discord," and predicted that trouble would come after he passed.

However, the Ridda Wars had only recently ended. Khalid ibn Walid[ra] and 'Ubayda[ra] had successfully conquered Damascus and much of Persia. Islam was now much wider spread and 'Umar[ra] had the huge task of establishing order and justice throughout the lands, as well as repelling future attacks by the Byzantines and Persians who were recovering from the shock of having lost a significant part of their territories to the Muslims.

DISMISSAL OF KHALID IBN WALID[ra]

One of the first things he did was to dismiss Khalid ibn Walid[ra] from his post as general of the Muslim army. Khalid, after so many successes, was becoming a celebrity amongst the Muslims and 'Umar[ra] feared that they would attribute success to Khalid ibn Walid, the Sword of Allah, rather than to Allah himself . 'Ubayda[ra] was given the post of the general of the Muslim army.

The people could not understand this decision, so 'Umar[ra] said to them, "I have not dismissed Khalid because of my anger or because of any dishonesty on his part, but because people glorified him and were misled. I feared that people would rely on him for victory. I want them to know that it is Allah who does all things, and there should be no mischief in the land."

Abu 'Ubayda[ra] as the commander of the army, gave Khalid[ra] the command of the cavalry and Khalid[ra] continued to achieve many victories. He accepted the decision of 'Umar[ra].

Image from Total War video game by Creative Assembly. Romans vs Persians

BYZANTINES AND PERSIANS

Even though the Byzantines and the Persians were an ongoing threat, 'Umar intended to consolidate and bring stable governorship to the areas that had already been conquered. However, work needed to be done in Syria, because although Damascus had been captured the year before in 634, the rest of Syria was still in question. There were various battles including Ablah, near Beirut, and Fahl, in the Jordan Valley, where the Byzantine army was defeated by Khalid's forces in January, 635.

Over the next five years, the Muslim army continued into Palestine, taking Caesarea in a long siege. Jewish people on the whole were relieved, as they were now allowed to pray and attend their temples under Muslim law.

The Muslims had to recapture Damascus and then moved on to Emesa in 636.

Khalid received information that Heraclius was planning to send a huge army of around 20,000. Heraclius decided to try to avoid pitched battles, due to past experience with the Muslims, so preferred to reinforce the major cities and try and devised a strategy to fragment the Muslim troops and then defeat them.

A STRATEGIC SUCCESS FOR THE MUSLIMS

Part of Heraclius's plan was to join forces with the Persians in one huge army against the Muslims, even though they had been long-standing enemies. However, 'Umar made a clever tactical manoeuvre and lured the Romans into battle before they could coordinate with the Persians.

He did this by engaging Yazdegerd III in negotiations, while sending reinforcements to the Roman front, to Yarmouk, with instructions that they should appear in the form of small bands, one after the other, giving the impression of a continuous stream of reinforcements that finally lured the Byzantines to be defeated.

Three months later, the Persian army was defeated in the Battle of Qadisiyyah.

There were further battles between the Muslims and the Byzantines in Syria, including the Battle of the Iron Bridge, resulting in the surrender of Antioch. The Muslims marched north of Syria and secured Armenia. As the whole of the region was now under Muslim control, this created a buffer zone between the Byzantine Empire and the Muslim-controlled lands which was what 'Umar had wanted, "I wish there was a wall of fire between us and the Romans, so that neither we could cross into their land, nor they could to ours."

'Umar did not want to continue further into Byzantine territory, even though his generals recommended it. He preferred to consolidate the new provinces and bring stability and peace.

In 637 after a two-month siege, the Muslims captured Ctesiphon, the Persian capital. This followed the victory at Qadisiyyah. Afterwards, they captured Tikrit and Mosul. The generals wanted to continue further east but 'Umar was happy to let the Zagros mountains act as a buffer between the Muslims and other lands as, "I prefer the safety of Muslims to the spoils of war."

Muslims were allowed to buy and sell property in foreign lands, like everyone else, but there was no permission for the unlawful use of houses or other property of those people.

However, 'Umar received reports that some soldiers in Syria were taking land and property for themselves on their conquests. He was angered by this and personally travelled all the way to Syria to oversee the return of the property to its original owners.

'UMAR'S HUMILITY

When the treasures of these lands poured into Medina, and the Muslims saw this wealth, they rejoiced. However, 'Umar wept. Someone said to him, "This is a day of thanks and joy, not a day of weeping." 'Umar replied, "By Allah, such as this wealth never became abundant among a people except it caused fighting between them." He then prayed to Allah for safety on this matter and ordered Suraqa b. Malik b. Ju'shum, a tall and very thin black Bedouin to wear the gold armlets and bracelets of the king of Persia, Chosroes. Suraqa began to say, "Allahu Akbar, Allahu Akbar!" He remembered that the Prophet ﷺ had said many years before, "I can see you wearing the armlets of Chosroes."

Jerusalem

Jerusalem is one of the oldest cities in the world and has always been a key city in the history of religion. The original City of Dawud (the Prophet David) was built here by King Sulayman (Soloman), the temple being revered by the Jewish faith. It is also home to the two most holy sites of Christianity: the place where Jesus was said to have been crucified and where he was said to have been buried and risen again. For the Muslims, Jerusalem is the third holiest site after Makkah and Medina, because Prophet Muhammad ﷺ ascended on the Night Journey from the Dome of the Rock after praying with all the other Prophets at Masjid al-Aqsa, and also because it had been the Muslims' first Qiblah.

During its long history, Jerusalem has been:

Destroyed at least twice

Besieged twenty-three times

Attacked fifty-two times

Captured and recaptured fourty-four times.

This means that Jerusalem is a city for which all faiths feel a great fondness and that they wish to govern themselves.

Due to the ongoing conflicts with the Byzantines, the Muslim army laid siege to Jerusalem in 637 AD and this was intentionally a siege without combat to avoid casualties.

This lasted for four months until the patriarch surrendered but on the condition that he met with the khalifah, Sayyidina 'Umar, personally.

'Umar was about sixty years old when he received the request. He was in Medina, which is where he liked to govern, but decided it was indeed a necessary mission. He left Medina and eventually arrived at Jerusalem with his servant, alternately walking and then

The Dome of the Rock in the Masjid al-Aqsa complex. The third holiest site in Islam.

St Sophronious, the Patriarch of Jerusalem

riding a camel that they shared, as was his practice. He was wearing simple, threadbare clothes. Some tried to get him to wear clothes that were more befitting to his position but he refused and said: *"We are a people that Allah has honoured us with Islam, if we seek it through anything else then Allah will humiliate us."*

He walked up to the gates without an armed guard, only with his servant. It happened to be the servant's turn to ride the donkey. 'Umar had also fallen into a muddy puddle so had stains on his white garments, but still did not turn back to the camp to change.

The Patriarch Sophronius was so impressed with the humble demeanour and greatness of this khalifah he said, "To a man like this, Jerusalem is handed over." And agreed to negotiate and eventually handed the keys to 'Umar in 637. As a condition, the patriarch had wanted Sayyidina 'Umar to refuse entry to Jewish people. Initially, 'Umar agreed, but soon reversed this decision as it was not in line with Islamic law.

Bishop Sophronius took 'Umar on a tour of the city including the Church of the Holy Sepulchre, when the time for prayer came Sophronius invited 'Umar to pray in the church but he declined, fearing the church would be converted to a mosque, thus depriving Christendom of one of its holiest sites. Instead, he prayed outside. Thus the Mosque of 'Umar was built opposite the Church of the Holy Sepulchre.

Sayyidina 'Umar then asked to be shown the place from which the Prophet Muhammad ﷺ ascended on his Night Journey. They found the area covered in rubbish, dust and rubble, so they cleaned it and set to work at once to build a mosque on the site: Masjid al-Aqsa (The Farthest Mosque).

Sayyidina 'Umar reversed the almost five hundred year Christian ban on Jews, and ordered his men to find eighty Jewish familes to settle there and allowed any others to return to Jerusalem. He granted Christians free use of their holy sites. Thus he turned Jerusalem into a city where Jews, Christians, and Muslims lived in tolerance, peace, and harmony.

Only Islam has a clear set of guidelines for those of other faiths that enables them to live side by side, in an atmosphere of respect and only under Muslim rule was Jerusalem a safe place for all faiths; where each faith had its temples and churches and self-governance according to their own laws.

This is the treaty between Sayyidina 'Umar and the people of Jerusalem which is still preserved in the Church of the Holy Sepulchre:

In the Name of God, the Merciful, the Compassionate, this is the assurance of safety that the servant of God, 'Umar, the Commander of the Faithful, has given to the people of Jerusalem. He has assured them of safety for themselves, their property, their churches, their crosses, the sick and healthy of the city and for all the rituals which belong to their religion. Their churches will not be inhabited by Muslims and will not be destroyed. Neither they, nor the land on which they stand, nor their cross, nor their property will be damaged. They will not be forcibly converted. The people of Jerusalem must pay the taxes like the people of other cities and must expel the Byzantines and the robbers. Those of the people of Jerusalem who want to leave with the Byzantines, take their property and abandon their churches and crosses will be safe until they reach their place of refuge. The villagers may remain in the city if they wish but must pay taxes like the citizens. Those who wish may go with the Byzantines and those who wish may return to their families. Nothing is to be taken from them before their harvest is reaped. If they pay their taxes according to their obligations, then the conditions laid out in this letter are under the covenant of God, are the responsibility of His Prophet, of the khulafah and of the faithful."

Conquest of Egypt

Caravan resting in the desert by by Ippolito Caffi

Egypt had been ruled by the Byzantine Empire for over six-hundred years. The Sassanid Empire managed to take control of the country in 618 but the Byzantines re-conquered it in 629, just four years before the Muslims arrived.

PERMISSION TO ATTACK

'Amr ibn al-'As* tried to persuade 'Umar* to invade Egypt with all its wealth and strategic positions. 'Umar* was reluctant, however, and said, "The life of one of my soldiers is dearer to me than a million dirham." The matter was pressed and went to parliament in Medina to decide. The parliament decided to send the army to Egypt in 639 because they knew that Egypt was a stronghold of the Byzantine Roman Empire and posed a threat from the West.

With only 4,000 men, joined by some Roman and Persian converts, 'Amr ibn al-'As* arrived at the borders of Egypt. Meanwhile 'Umar* was still concerned about the expedition and wrote a letter to 'Amr ibn al'As* telling him to return to Medina unless he was already on Egyptian soil. 'Amr* guessed the contents of the letter and delayed opening it until the army was in Egypt and thus continued on.

When 'Umar* heard, he at once began to prepare more troops to send to Egypt from Medina as he knew 'Amr* would need a lot more men to safely conquer the area.

EL ARISH, PELSIUM AND BELBEIS

On Eid al-Adha, the Muslim army marched to El Arish, which had no garrison and took the town easily, the inhabitants agreeing to the usual terms.

Meanwhile, the daughter of Cyrus of Alexandria, the Patriarch, heard of the invasion and dispatched a regiment of her soldiers to defend Pelusium, considered to be the gateway to Egypt.

In January 640 the Muslims arrived and laid siege which lasted two months. Finally, Hudhayfah ibn Wala, with a small team captured the city.

Two Bedouin tribes, the Rashidah and Lakhm, joined the Muslim army, increasing their numbers.

At Belbeis, 'Amr* was met by two Christian monks, Cyrus and the famous Roman general, Aretion, to negotiate. They were given the three usual choices and they took five days to reflect. Cyrus wanted to agree to the terms but the others did not. The resulting battle was a Muslim victory and then a siege on the city of Belbeis which fell about a month later.

BABYLON

So far, the conquest had taken a lot longer than 'Amr̊ had predicted. They now arrived at Babylon, a far bigger city with huge, eighteen-meter walls which were two metres thick. The Romans were prepared for the siege and all attempts to take Babylon ended in failure.

Still in seige, 'Amr̊ sent troops to surrounding towns, some of which they took. They killed a Roman general, John, who had been following them. When news of his death reached the commander of the army at Babylon, he was greatly saddened "His lamentations were more grievous than the lamentations of David over Saul when he said: 'How have the mighty fallen, and the weapons of war perished!'"

REINFORCEMENTS

'Amr̊ was now concerned about the progress and sent a request for more troops, but they were already on their way. These were the elite of the Muslim army with Zubayr ibn al-Awwam̊ as the commander. As they arrived, some Roman soldiers refused to fight saying "We have a small chance against the men who have conquered Chosroes and Caesar in Syria."

HELIOPOLIS AND FAYOUM

When he arrived, Zubayr̊ pointed out to 'Amr̊ that attacking the city of Heliopolis would help the siege of Babylon, as the Romans would have to send troops to defend it.

Heliopolis is the great city of the Pharaohs with its huge Sun Temple.

The two armies fought and the Romans were pushed back to Babylon.

When the governor of Fayoum heard of the fall of Heliopolis, he abandoned the city and so did the governor of Abuit.

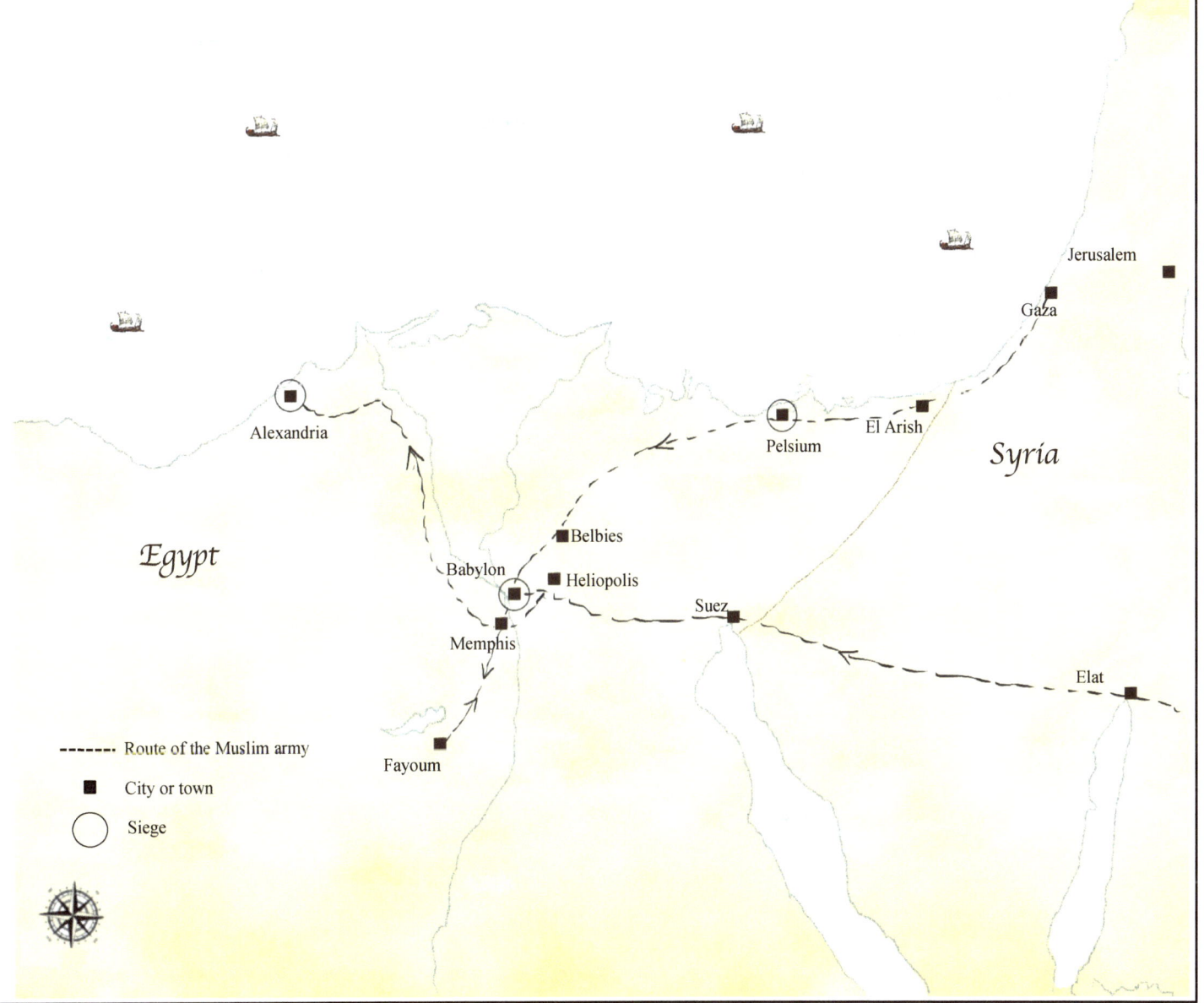

------- Route of the Muslim army

■ City or town

◯ Siege

Ancient Alexandria by Adolf Gnauth 1878

NEGOTIATIONS WITH CYRUS

After failed attempts by the Romans in Babylon to attack the Muslims across the siege ditch, they began negotiations with Cyrus. 'Amr* then met with Theodorus but after negotiations stalled, Zubayr* led a small garrison into the city walls and opened the gates.

In all the siege had lasted seven months.

Cyrus sent an envoy to 'Amr* saying that they will be far outnumbered when the full force of Byzantium arrives and that they are surrounded by the Nile, so defeat is certain. Of course, 'Amr* was not easily worried about this and invited the envoy to stay a few days to observe the Muslims and sent him back with the usual choices. The envoy reported back and said "We have seen a people who prefer death to life and humility to pride. They sit in the dust, and they take their meals on horseback. Their commander is one of themselves: there is no distinction of rank among them. They have fixed hours of prayer at which all pray, first washing their hands and feet, and they pray with reverence."

On another meeting with Cyrus, 'Amr* sent Ubadah ibn al-Samit*, a black man. When Cyrus saw Ubadah* he said; "I will have no meeting with him! Take away that black man." But the Muslims explained that Ubadah* was one of their most trusted generals. Ubadah said; "There are a thousand blacks, as black as myself, among our companions. I and they would be ready each to meet and fight a hundred enemies together. We live only to fight for God, and to follow His will. We care nought for wealth, so long as we have the wherewithal to stay our hunger and to clothe our bodies. This world is nothing to us." Moved by this, Cyrus turned to his companions and said "Do you hear this? I much fear that God has sent these men to take over the world." Cyrus offered, on behalf of the Romans, to pay off the Muslim army with a very generous settlement as long as they would return home. But this was rejected and the same terms were offered.

Cyrus and the officials again deliberated and considered accepting Islam but decided; "We cannot abandon the religion of Christ for a religion of which we know nothing." So they chose submission and tribute. So on 22nd December 641, the Muslims were the rulers of all of Egypt, according to Cyrus.

Heraclius was furious however, refused to accept the decision, insulted Cyrus, and looked forward to joining the 100,000 troops in the defense of Egypt, who were soon ready to leave.

ALEXANDRIA

After some difficulties on the way, the Muslim army arrived at Alexandria in March 641. The city of Alexandria had walls within walls and forts within forts. The city was next to the sea so could be re-supplied from Constantinople. A siege would prove difficult.

The Romans fired catapults from the city walls that bombarded the Muslims and so they were forced to camp quite far from the walls. Various attacks were made by the Romans but were repelled.

In Constantinople, where the huge army was being gathered, Heraclius was preparing to leave with the army. However, by the Will of Allah, he died, leaving the army in some chaos due to a succession crisis.

When no reinforcements arrived, those defending Alexandria were demoralised but continued on so that the siege lasted six months. 'Umar*, concerned about the length of time, instructed 'Ubaydah to take charge who then led an attack which led to the capture of Alexandria.

Egpyt was now fully under Muslim control.

CYRUS OF ALEXANDRIA

Around this time, most of Egypt followed Coptic Christitianity. There were many other branches believing different things about Christ, if he was God on earth, or if he had two natures. Cyrus of Alexandria followed a branch called monotheletism (not to be confused with monotheism) and was given the post of the See of Alexandia in 630 by Pope Honotious I in Rome to ensure the peoples of Egypt followed this branch of Christianity.

For 10 years, Cyrus severely persecuted the Egyptians, attempting to bring them, by force if necessary, to his faith. The majority of the Egyptian people did not recognise him as patriarch, instead recognising Pope Benjamin I who had gone into hiding and was relentlessly hunted by Cyrus, though without success. On one occasion, Cyrus's troops seized Benjamin's brother Menas and burned him with torches until, 'the fat dropped down from both his sides to the ground'. Still unshaken, his teeth were pulled out, and he was stuffed into a sack filled with sand and taken by a boat seven bowshots away from the shore. Three times he was offered his life if he accepted the Council of Chalcedon, and three times he refused, before he was thrown into the sea and drowned. "Yet it was not they who were victorious over Menas, that champion of the faith, but Menas who by Christian patience overcame them," says the biographer of Benjamin.

Cyrus appointed Chalcedonian bishops over every Egyptian city, putting Coptic priests to death whenever they were found. The Coptic people, though left without priests, had secret gatherings.

Cyrus was a controversial figure and was despised by Rome who blamed him for allowing the Muslims to take Egypt and by the Coptic Christians who had been so persecuted.

He is sometimes confused in Islamic history with al-Muqawqis, the Coptic ruler, who offered sanctuary to the early Muslims but this was before Cyrus was given the post of patriarch and was quite a different personality.

POPE BENJAMIN I

Pope Benjamin I is considered a saint and one of the greatest patriarchs of the Coptic church and a very ascetic and pious man. 'Amr described him as 'an impressive man of God' and met with him a number of times.

Some reports say that Benjamin assisted 'Amr and the Muslims, perhaps because he respected the Muslims or because it was a way to remove Cyrus and would allow them to pray freely under Muslim rule.

THE STORY OF THE NILE RIVER

When 'Amr ibn al-'As arrived after Egypt was conquered, he discovered a strange practice. The people told him that every year, they had to select a young virgin girl with the consent of her parents, dress her in fine garments and throw her into the Nile. If they did not do this, they believed that the Nile would not rise and the crops would fail. It was about that time of year so 'Amr ibn al-'As forbade it saying, "This can never be in Islam, and Islam destroys the bad practices that came before it."

The ritual was not performed, and the Nile did not rise very much. The people were getting restless and wanted to expel 'Amr ibn al-As. 'Amr wrote to 'Umar, who wrote back to say that he had done the correct thing and enclosed another note, to be given to the Nile river. It said:

"From the servant of Allah, the Prince of the Faithful to the Nile of Egypt. Now if you rose by your own power then rise not, but if the Lord caused you to rise, then I implore the Lord, the One, the Conqueror, to make you rise!"

'Amr cast this paper into the Nile the day before the Festival of the Cross and amazingly the river rose sixteen cubits in one night (approx. eight metres). This put an end to the custom.

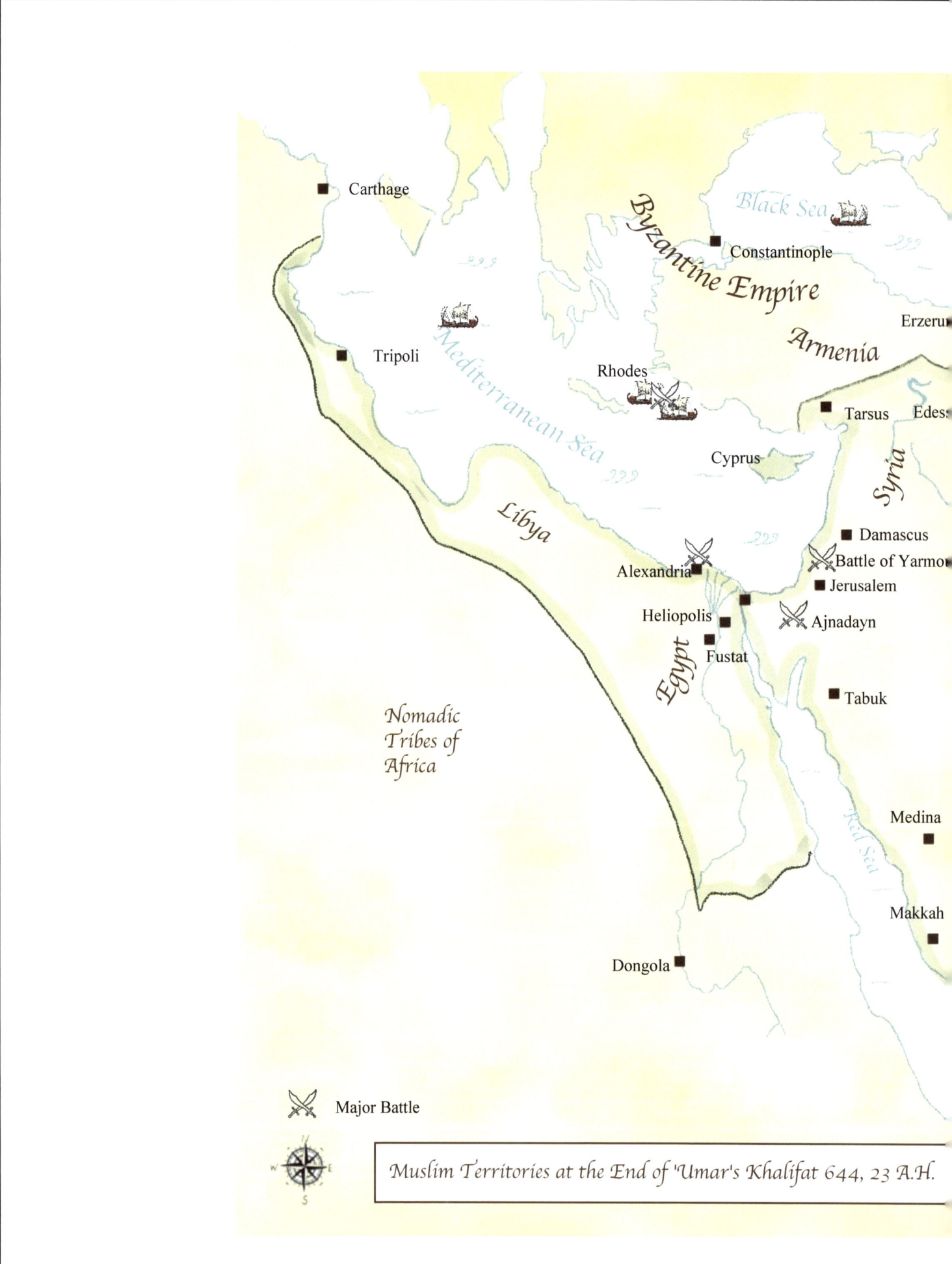

Carthage

Black Sea

Byzantine Empire

Constantinople

Armenia

Erzeru

Tripoli

Mediterranean Sea

Rhodes

Tarsus

Edes:

Syria

Cyprus

Libya

Damascus

Battle of Yarmo

Alexandria

Jerusalem

Heliopolis

Ajnadayn

Egypt

Fustat

Tabuk

Nomadic
Tribes of
Africa

Medina

Red Sea

Makkah

Dongola

Major Battle

Muslim Territories at the End of 'Umar's Khalifat 644, 23 A.H.

Tiflis

Caspian Sea

Azerbaijan

Transoxiana

Samarkand

Bukhara

Balkh

Tabriz

Kabul

Mosul

Herat

Nehavend

Baghdad

Ctesiphon

Qadisiyyah

Isfahan

Seistan

Kufa

Basra

Istakhr

Makran

Persian Gulf

Sind

Arabia

Oman

Najran

Indian Ocean

Yemen

The Martydom of 'Umar

Gathering around the fallen Khalifah by Hana Horack-Elyafi

One night, 'Umar had a dream that a bird struck him two or three times in his chest and he said that he felt something of his death.

On 31st October 644 (22 A.H.), Sayyidina 'Umar was leading the Fajr prayers, when a man came up behind him and stabbed him six times in the belly. 'Umar tried three times to stand to continue the prayer but collapsed each time. People flooded around him and others caught the attacker who wounded twelve (of which many later died) other Muslims until the attacker committed suicide by stabbing himself.

'Umar lost conciousness as he was brought to the nearest house. When he woke a little, the first thing he asked was if the jumaat finished the fajr prayer and was relieved when he heard they had. He then asked his son, 'Abd Allah, to go to Sayyidatina 'Aisha's house and give greetings from 'Umar, (not as the khalifah but as a friend of the Prophet ﷺ) with his humble request to be buried next to the Prophet ﷺ and Abu Bakr. 'Aisha was found crying in her room. Her touching reply was, "I had the idea of having this place for myself, but today I swear I will indeed prefer 'Umar to myself."

WHO WAS THE ATTACKER?

The assassin was said to be a Persian slave named Piruz Nahavandi or Abu Lulu. His motivation for the assassination is not clear and there are two possible versions:

One is that the assassination was planned several months earlier, possibly by Hormuzna, a disloyal Persian chief who had pretended to accept Islam.

The other version describes Abu Lulu who entered Medina as a non-Muslim, but a skilled weapons maker. Usually, non-Muslims were not allowed to live in Medina but Abu Lulu was given special permission and asked to pay a higher tax on his craft. He was not happy about this and threatened 'Umar, even though 'Umar was very lenient with him. Abu Lulu's resentments may have grown, making him decide to assasinate him.

THE PASSING TO THE NEXT LIFE

Sayyidina 'Umar died of the wounds on Wednesday 3 November 644 (26th Dhū al-Ḥijja 23). As per 'Umar's request, he was buried alongside the Prophet Muhammad ﷺ and Abu Bakr as Siddique by the permission of 'Aisha.

Like the Prophet Muhammad ﷺ, Abu Bakr as-Siddique was 63 years old when he passed to the next life.

"Islam is today rent," said Umm Ayman.

Abdul Rahman al-Yassir reported, "I witnessed the death of 'Umar, and the sun was eclipsed on that day."

The Prophet ﷺ had said, "Jibrael said to me, 'Truly Islam will weep at the death of 'Umar.'" (Ubayy ibn Kaa'b).

The Prophet ﷺ also said, "He who hates 'Umar, hates me, and he who loves 'Umar, loves me, and the Lord gloried regarding the people at Arafat in general and rejoiced over 'Umar in particular, and the Lord has never sent a prophet, but there was among his people one inspired, and if there be one among my people, it is 'Umar."

The people asked, 'How inspired?' and the Prophet ﷺ said, 'The angels speak by his tongue.'"

The time ahead was not going to be an easy one. The Prophet ﷺ predicted that the Khalifa after 'Umar would be 'killed by a cruel faction' and after that 'shall follow calamity'.

THE NEXT KHALIFAH?

'Umar considered who should succeed him as the khalifah, and he said he would have appointed Mu'adh ibn Jabal or Abu 'Ubaydah ibn Jarrah or Khalid ibn Walid if they were still alive. Instead, 'Umar appointed a committee of six persons comprising 'Abdur Rahman bin 'Awf, Saad ibn Abi Waqqas, Talha ibn 'Ubaydullah, 'Uthman ibn Affan, 'Ali ibn Abi Talib, and Zubayr ibn al-Awwam. These men were amongst the ten people promised Paradise by the Prophet Muhammad ﷺ. They later decided it was to be 'Uthman ibn Afwan who would be the next khalif of Islam.

Sayyidina 'Umar is buried next to the Prophet Muhammad ﷺ and Sayyidina Abu Bakr as Siddique in the Masjid an-Nabawi, Medina, Saudi Arabia.

Famous Quotes of Sayyidina 'Umar
The Prince of the Faithful - Amir al-Mu'mineen

"One sees minor faults of others but overlooks his own major faults."

"I have never regretted my silence, but I have regretted my speech many times."

"The best way to defeat someone is to beat them at politeness."

"If something is meant to be elsewhere, it will never reach you, but if it is yours by destiny, then from it you cannot flee."

"Stick to the truth, even if the truth kills you."

"Women are not a garment you wear and undress however you like. They are honoured and have rights."

"A man should be like a child with his wife, but if she needs him, he should act like a man."

"Get used to a rough life, because luxury does not last forever."

"The person who calls himself learned, indeed he is ignorant, and the one who calls himself from the dwellers of Paradise surely he is from the dwellers of Hell."

"No amount of guilt can change the past and no amount of worrying can change the future."

"Whoever shows you your faults is your friend. Those that pay you lip service in praise are your executioners."

"Sit with those who have sinned and repented for they have the softest of hearts."

"We were the most humiliated people on Earth and Allah gave us honour through Islam. If we ever seek honour through anything else, Allah will again humiliate us."

"Avoidance of sin is lighter than the pain of remorse."

"Hold on to your prayer (salat), because if you lose that, you will lose everything else."

"I fear a day when the disbelievers are proud of their falsehood, and the Muslims are shy of their faith."

"'Invite people to Islam even without words.' They asked 'How?' 'With your manners.'"

"Sometimes people with the worst past, create the best future."

"Learn before you become leaders!"

"We found that the goodness of our lives was patience."

Sayyidina 'Uthman ibn Affan ؓ

Sayyidina 'Uthman ؓ was the son-in-law of the Prophet Muhammad ﷺ, one of the first to accept Islam and the fourth male to embrace Islam, after 'Ali bin Abi Talib , Abu Bakr and Zayd bin Thabit.

He was the first one to make a standardised copy of the Qur'an and he was one of the ten to whom the attainment of Paradise was promised and one of the six whom when he died, the Prophet ﷺ was well pleased with.

The Prophet Muhammad ﷺ said;

"'Uthman is the possessor of two Luminaries"

"Every prophet has a companion in Paradise. My companion there is 'Uthman."

"'Uthman most resembles me in disposition."

"Truly the angels are shy in the presence of 'Uthman as they are shy before Allah and His Messenger."

"The most compassionate towards my community is Abu Bakr; the staunchest in the Religion of Allah is 'Umar; and the most truthful in his virtue is 'Uthman."

'Uthman was alluded to in the Qur'an;

"Those that spend their wealth in the way of the One God then do not follow up what they spend with reminders of past favours and with harm: theirs are wages with their nurturing Lord, and they have nothing to fear, and they shall not grieve." (al-Baqara 2:262)

"Of the believers are men who are true to what they promised with the One God. Of them is he who has fulfilled his solemn pledge, and of them is he that awaits. And they never altered with any alteration." (al-Ahzab 33:23)

His Early Life

'Uthman was born in Ta'if seven years after the Prophet Muhammad ﷺ. His father was Affan ibn Abi al-'As, of the Umayyad clan, and his mother was Arwa bint Kurayz, of the 'Abd ash-Shams. Arwa's mother was Umm Hakim bint 'Abdul Muttalib, making Arwa the first cousin of Muhammad and 'Uthman his first cousin's son. 'Uthman had one sister, Amina.

'Uthman was part of the powerful Umayyad clan, the most wealthy and influential of the Quraysh. 'Uthman was their 'golden child', their most beloved, because of his good manners and shyness. He was also very generous, giving to those in need. He also learned how to read and write which was rare in those days.

His father, Affan, died at a young age while travelling abroad, leaving 'Uthman with a large inheritance. He became a merchant like his father, and his business flourished, making him one of the richest men among the Quraysh. 'Uthman had a high social and economic standing, yet he was always modest and humble in character.

'UTHMAN'S CONVERSION TO ISLAM

In 611, 'Uthman returned home after a long business trip and heard about the new religion that Muhammad ﷺ was preaching. 'Uthman went to Abu Bakr whom he knew to be a close friend of Muhammad's ﷺ and Abu Bakr told him what the new faith was about - urging people to reject the false worship of idols and to accept the belief in Allah as the One God. 'Uthman, whose heart was open went to Muhammad ﷺ. The Prophet ﷺ welcomed 'Uthman and told him of his experience in Mount Hira when he received the first revelation. 'Uthman was excited to hear this and he recounted his dream that he had heard in Syria, "O sleeper, get up, for Ahmad has emerged in Makkah." The Prophet ﷺ stretched out his hand, which 'Uthman grasped in reverence, and declared, "There is no God but Allah, and Muhammad is His Prophet." 'Uthman was thirty-four years old and was one of the earliest Muslims.

'Uthman's family, however, were enraged that their favourite son had betrayed them. Perhaps because all their hopes were pinned on him, they treated him very badly trying to get him to

Edwin Lord Weeks - Arrival of a Caravan Outside the City of Morocco

Muslims conversing with the Negus of Abyssinia

renounce his new religion. His uncle shackled him and locked him in a small room and refused to release him until he gave up the religion, which 'Uthman refused to do. After a long time, he was set free as it was clear he would not submit to their demands.

'Uthman hoped his wives would also accept Islam, but they refused and continued to worship the idols. He then felt he must divorce them which he was sad about. However, the Prophet ﷺ, knowing that 'Uthman had such a kind and sweet nature and was very pious, offered his daughter, the beautiful Sayyidah Ruyayya for his wife, with her acceptance. 'Uthman also joyously accepted. It is said that 'Uthman and Ruqayya made a unique pair, as 'Uthman was the most handsome person amongst the men and Ruqayya was the most beautiful amongst the women. When 'Usama ibn Zayd was sent on an errand to their house, he found himself staying to stare at her and at 'Uthman in turns, delaying his return. Muhammad ﷺ knew why he had been delayed and asked 'Usama, "Have you ever seen a more handsome couple than those two?" and he agreed that he had not.

MIGRATION

The Prophet ﷺ knew of a just king, the Negus of Abyssinia, and advised the Muslims to travel there to seek shelter in 615, because of the continued torture and oppression. Among those who travelled there were 'Uthman and his wife, Ruqayya, ten men and two women. 'Uthman set up a business there quite easily as he had some contacts in the region and his business did well for the two years that they were there.

After four years, some news spread among the Muslims in Abyssinia that the Quraysh of Makkah had accepted Islam, which persuaded 'Uthman, Ruqayya and the now thirty-nine Muslims to return. However, when they reached Makkah, they found that the news about the Quraysh's acceptance of Islam was false and that in fact the Muslims had remained oppressed and their living conditions had worsened. The Quraysh had decided to cut all social, economic, and familial relations with the Muslims and Bani Hashim (the Prophet's ﷺ clan). They were banished and prevented from leaving their valley. They were deprived of a reasonable living so they did not even have sufficient food and water. It was a fortunate thing that 'Uthman had returned, as he immediately ordered food and supplies and secretly gave them to the Muslims.

His business, although having to start afresh and despite the situation in Makkah, continued to do very well.

In 622, when the Prophet ﷺ migrated to Medina, the Muslims were invited to join the Prophet ﷺ and escape the continual harsh treatment and of course, 'Uthman and Ruqayyah joined them.

Conditions in Medina were not easy, however, as many Muslims had to leave their worldly possessions behind and relied on the support of the Ansar.

His Character and Generosity During the Time of the Prophet

Sayyidina 'Uthman was known to be a very truthful man with a modest character. 'Uthman did not seek entertainment and songs and other material pleasures. He was a man of high principles and morals and possessed pure thoughts and actions.

He was also well known for his shyness. It was narrated that Prophet Muhammad ﷺ was reclining in his house while part of his leg was uncovered. Abu Bakr sought permission to enter, so he permitted him to enter and spoke to him. 'Umar bin Al-Khattab sought permission to enter, so he permitted him to enter and spoke to him. Then 'Uthman bin Affan sought permission to enter, so the Prophet ﷺ sat up and straightened his garments. 'Uthman was then permitted to enter and he spoke to him.

When 'Uthman left, 'Aisha, the Prophet's ﷺ wife, asked, "Abu Bakr came and you did not move, 'Umar came and you did not move, but when 'Uthman came, you sat up and straightened your garments?"

The Prophet ﷺ replied, "Should I not feel shy before a man from whom the angels feel shy?" (Sahih Muslim)

He was mild-mannered, kind, and considerate as well as very pious. As a true and generous believer, he was known for his great desire to please Allah and sacrifice all his trade and property for the support of Islam. 'Uthman was known to fast the whole year and spend the night in prayer except for a rest in its first part and perform Hajj every year. 'Uthman knew the Qur'an from memory and was known to have had an intimate knowledge of the context and circumstances in which each verse had been related.

Even though he was wealthy, 'Uthman maintained a lifestyle devoid of luxury and the pursuit of worldly possessions. Such was his humility that he was known to have often slept on bare sand in the courtyard of the Prophet's mosque.

It has been said that 'Uthman's generosity could not be surpassed by anyone, except Abu Bakr. As well as significant contributions made towards the cause of Islam, 'Uthman took it upon himself to give alms and look after widows and orphans. It was also customary for him to free a slave every Friday.

The ḥūrīs and inhabitants of Paradise. Anonymous, Miʿrājnāma (Book of Ascension). Probably Herat, circa 1436. Bibliothèque Nationale de France, Paris.

A TERRIBLE DROUGHT

Repeatedly, 'Uthman's generosity saved the Muslims during difficult times. One year, under the Khalifah of 'Umar bin Al-Khattab, there had been no rainfall, crops shriveled and died, and there was a severe shortage of food. A caravan of one thousand camels laden with grains and supplies had just arrived from Syria, and it belonged to 'Uthman. Merchants raced to 'Uthman to negotiate a deal. They offered to buy the grains at a 5% profit for 'Uthman, but he turned them down, claiming that he found a better offer. He already had an offer of ten times the profit; for every dirham he spent in charity, Allah would reward him tenfold and up to seven hundred times more. 'Uthman distributed the entire stock of food grains among the poor people, free of charge.

TABUK

The ninth year after Hijrah saw the Prophet ﷺ preparing an army for battle with the Romans who were plotting to disrupt the expanding territories of the Khilafah. With limited resources and the near-impossible task of adequately equipping the army in the middle of a very hot summer, the Prophet ﷺ sought the assistance of his companions to donate as much as they could. 'Uthman immediately obliged and was credited to have provided nine hundred and forty camels along with sixty horses for the Tabuk expedition. He had also given ten thousand dinars to the Prophet ﷺ to ensure that the army was well equipped. The Prophet ﷺ remarked, "Whatever 'Uthman does from this day onward, he will suffer no harm."

EXPANSION OF THE PROPHET'S MOSQUE

When the number of converts to Islam increased in Medina, the mosque became full. The Prophet ﷺ hoped that perhaps one of his Companions could help with the purchase of the neighbouring area to facilitate the expansion of the mosque and said, "Who will buy the land of so and so and add it to the mosque in return for something good for him in Paradise?" 'Uthman was only to willing to oblige and proceeded to the owners of this area with an offer to purchase.

Later, when the Prophet ﷺ returned from their victorious campaign in Makkah, he sought to once again expand the area of the sacred mosque. He suggested that the owners of the home beside the mosque donate it, but they did not, saying that they had nothing else to their name and no other means of finding another home. 'Uthman then came forward and purchased a house for the owners, an even larger one than they had given up.

SUPPORTING THE UMMAH

During the rule of Abu Bakr, the Muslims underwent great hardships, one of which was food scarcity. As a merchant, 'Uthman received a substantial delivery of food and other goods from Damascus, and he donated the entire caravan to the poor to help them survive the harsh conditions. This generosity never diminished his wealth. With hard work and honesty, his business flourished, making him one of the richest men in Medina.

19th Century Lithograph of an Arab well

THE WELL

Once, shortly after the Muslims migrated to Medina, water was scarce; they needed a source of drinking water. There was only one well in their near vicinity, which was owned by a Jewish man who used to charge the Muslims a high price to use the well. Living conditions were becoming increasingly difficult without water.

Prophet Muhammad ﷺ asked who could buy the well and dedicate it to the Muslims, and in return earn the reward of a house in Paradise.

'Uthman bin Affan was the first to come forward. He approached the Jewish man to buy the well, but the man rejected 'Uthman's offer. He would sell only half of the well to 'Uthman, for a large amount of money. 'Uthman accepted. The Muslims could fill water on alternate days, one day it was 'Uthman's turn and the next day it was the Jewish man's turn. On 'Uthman's day, he gave out the water for free to everybody. Naturally, nobody came to fill the water on the Jewish man's day, so he eventually sold the other half of the well to 'Uthman, due to lack of business. 'Uthman bin Affan dedicated the well to the people for free, and it continues to supply water even to this day.

THE POSSESSOR OF TWO LIGHTS

'Uthmans' beloved wife, Ruqayya, was taken ill at the time when the Muslims went to war at Badr. 'Uthman wanted to stay by her side as the Prophet ﷺ had permitted him to do, and so he is counted as one of the men of Badr. She passed to the next life during the battle.

Deeply grieved by the loss of Ruqayya, 'Uthman was asked by the Prophet ﷺ to marry his other daughter, Umm Kulthum. When she too passed away six years later, the Prophet ﷺ noted 'Uthman's grief in his manner of walking and expression on his face and said, "Had we a third daughter, surely, we would have given her in marriage to you."

It has been said that marriage to two daughters of the Prophet ﷺ earned 'Uthman the nickname Dhun-Noorayn (the one with the two lights); no one else had the privilege of having the Prophet ﷺ as a father-in-law twice over.

A WEDDING GIFT

When 'Ali married Fatima, 'Uthman bought 'Ali's shield for five hundred dirhams, even though it was only worth a tiny fraction of that. Four hundred was set aside as mahr (dower) for Fatima's marriage, leaving a hundred for all other expenses. Later, 'Uthman presented the armour back to 'Ali as a wedding present.

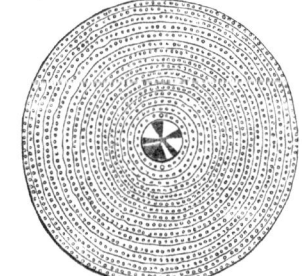

'Uthman﷿ as Khalifah

In 644, upon the nomination of the council organised by 'Umar﷿, 'Uthman﷿ became Khalifah. He was sixty-four years old.

After receiving the pledge of allegiance, he stood up and said:

"This world implies vanities, so let not the world mislead you and let no deceiver seduce you. Treat this world as Allah deals with it, and seek for the hereafter, for Allah gives an example of this world when He said, 'Set forth to the similitude of the life of this world, it is like the rain which We send down from the skies: the earth's vegetation absorbs it, but soon it becomes dry stubble, which the winds do scatter. It is only Allah who prevails over all things. Wealth and sons are allurements of the life of this world but the things that endure, good deeds, are best in the sight of thy Lord, as rewards, and the best foundation for hopes."

With the experience of his travels and his generosity and kind nature, 'Uthman﷿ was initially loved by the Muslims and during the first half of 'Uthman's﷿ reign, the Muslim world enjoyed internal peace and tranquillity, as well as economic prosperity.

He continued the social policies of those before him but relaxed some measures, including being able to buy and sell land in foreign countries. This meant there were more business opportunities.

In his Khalifah, Sayyidina 'Umar﷿ had been very strict in the use of money from the public treasury—indeed, apart from the meagre allowance that had been sanctioned in his favour, 'Umar took no money from the treasury. He did not receive any gifts, nor did he allow any of his family members to accept any gifts from any quarter. During the time of 'Uthman﷿, the restrictions on gifts were relaxed. 'Uthman﷿ did not receive a personal allowance from the treasury, nor did he receive a salary, as he was a wealthy man with sufficient resources of his own, but, unlike 'Umar﷿, 'Uthman﷿ accepted gifts and allowed his family members to do likewise from certain quarters.

'Uthman﷿ honestly expressed that he had the right to utilise the public funds according to his best judgement, and no one criticised him for that. The economic reforms introduced by 'Uthman﷿ had far-reaching effects; Muslims, as well as non-Muslims of the Rashidun Empire, enjoyed an economically prosperous life during his khalifate.

Arab market scene by E. Curry

EXPANSION OF THE PROPHET'S ﷺ MOSQUE

In the year 29 A.H., 'Uthman* added to and expanded the Prophet's ﷺ Mosque, adding beautifully carved stone walls, pillars of engraved stone and a teak roof.

COMPILING THE QUR'AN

'Uthman* was an expert in Qur'an and loved it deeply. He related that when the Companions and himself memorised the Qur'an, they spent time with the Prophet ﷺ to understand the full meanings. They would learn ten verses at a time and not move on until they had learned the knowledge contained within the verses.

In about AD 650, (25 AH) 'Uthman Hudhayfah ibn al-Yaman came to 'Uthman*. Hudhayfah was afraid of the differences in the recitation of the Qur'an among the people of Sham and Iraq, so he said to 'Uthman, "O Commander of the Faithful! Save this nation before they differ about the Book (Qur'an), as Jews and the Christians did before"

Slight differences in pronunciation of the Qur'an were noticed elsewhere too, as Islam expanded beyond the Arabian Peninsula into Persia, the Levant, and North Africa. To preserve the accurate pronunciation, 'Uthman* ordered a committee headed by Zayd ibn Thabit* to use the one copy that

This is said to be 'Uthman's personal copy of the Qur'an

had been compiled by Abu Bakr* to prepare a standardised Qur'an. 'Uthman* asked Hafsah* for this copy and he charged the following scribes to compile additional copies of it: Zayd bin Thabit*, 'Abdullah ibn al-Zubayr*, Sa'ad ibn al-As*, and 'Abdur Rahman ibn al-Harith*. They scribed at least four copies of the Qur'an, the exact number is not known. The original copy was returned to Hafsah*. One copy was sent to each major region of the empire, one remained in Medinah and he ordered any other versions or notes to be destroyed. Thus the standard copy of the Qur'anic text came into being. The Mushaf al-'Uthmani is considered the master copy of the Qur'anic text from which all subsequent authentic copies of the Qur'an have been made.

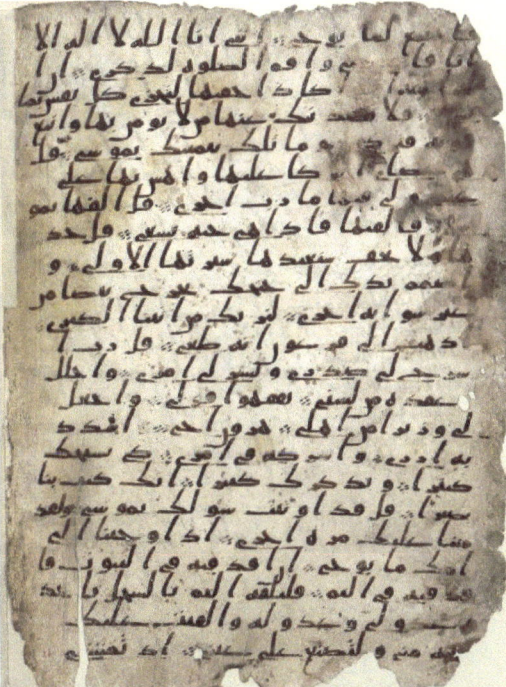

These fragments of the Qur'an, written on sheep or goat skin, were discovered at the university of Birmingham, U.K. and are considered the oldest in the world, dating back possibly to the time of the Prophet ﷺ and certainly during the time of 'Uthman. It is quite probable that whoever wrote the sacred verses personally knew the Prophet Muhammad ﷺ and this could have been one of the pages that Abu Bakr used to compile the first Qur'an.

This fragment contains parts of Suras from 18-20.

Military

In battle, 'Uthman was not an outstanding warrior and he was not given any military positions by the Prophet Muhammad ﷺ. However, under 'Uthman's leadership, the Muslim territories continued to expand as far west as Southern Spain and as far east as Sindh in Pakistan.

Although not a man of the battlefield, 'Uthman was skilled in conflict management. He effectively dealt with the heated and troubled early Muslim colonies, such as Kufa and Basra, by directing the hot-headed Arab settlers to new military campaigns and expansions which ended potential uprisings.

CARE OF THE EMPIRE

Upon his appointment, 'Uthman sent letters to his governors outlining his proposed policies and reminding them that as rulers, they must have excellent conduct and that their role is to protect society and not become tax collectors. The interest of all Muslims should be taken to heart and even with the enemies, their conduct should be upright.

During his rule, 'Uthman gave many of the top positions in government to his kinsmen such as 'Abdullah ibn Aamir, kept Mu'awiyah and 'Abdullah ibn Sa'ad ibn Abi as-Sarah. 'Uthman also gave the governors quite a lot of their own power to decide upon matters, unlike 'Umar who controlled things himself from Medina. By letting other governors make their own decisions, the Empire continued to expand rapidly. However, these policies also led to problems.

The sword of 'Uthman. The sword is 98 cm long and weighs alomst one kg. Its hilt is made of black stone and the cross guard is engraved with gold with floral

EGYPT AND CYPRUS

Hala Sultan Tekke, Cyprus

In 651 (31 A.H.), 'Uthman sent 'Abdullah ibn Zubayr and 'Abdullah ibn Saad to reconquer the Maghreb regions (North Africa at that time), where he met the army of Gregory the Patrician, Exarch of Africa and relative of Heraclius. That army is recorded to have numbered between 120,000 to 200,000 soldiers. The opposing forces clashed at Sabuthilag (or Sufetula), which became the name of this battle. Records from al-Bidayah w'al-Nihayah state that 'Abdullah's troops were surrounded by Gregory's army. However, 'Abdullah ibn Zubayr spotted Gregory in his chariot and asked 'Abdullah ibn Sa'd to lead a small detachment to intercept him. The interception was successful, and Gregory was slain by Zubayr's ambush party. Consequently, the morale of the Byzantine army crumbled and they were soon routed.

The Muslim army first arrived in Cyprus in 649, under the leadership of Mu'awiyah, and conquered the capital Salamis - Constantia after a short siege. Many of the local Catholic and Greek Orthodox Cypriots converted to Islam.

Umm Haram, an aunt of the Prophet Muhammad ﷺ, is buried there at the Hala Sultan Tekke monument. She had accompanied the navy for the expedition but while visiting the salt lake at Larnaka, sadly she fell off her horse and died.

FORMATION OF THE MUSLIM NAVY

One of the major additions to the Muslim army was a fleet of warships. This fleet could stand up to the impressive Byzantine fleet that dominated the Mediterranean seas in those days. 'Uthman* ordered Mu'awiyah bin Abi Sufyan, the governor of Syria and 'Abdullah ibn Saad*, the governor of North Africa to build the navy. Under the leadership of 'Abdullah ibn Saad*, coasts as far as Spain were explored as well as Rhodes and Cyprus which came under Muslim rule.

The Battle of the Masts in 655, against the Byzantines, off the coast of present-day Turkey, was the first major sea battle for the Muslims and ended in a huge victory, but with significant losses on each side.

The navy was also able to repel Byzantine attacks in Alexandria in 646.

The Muslim navy eventually became an impressive force as shown in this painting of the Ottoman fleet achored near the Ortakoy Mosque, Istanbul.

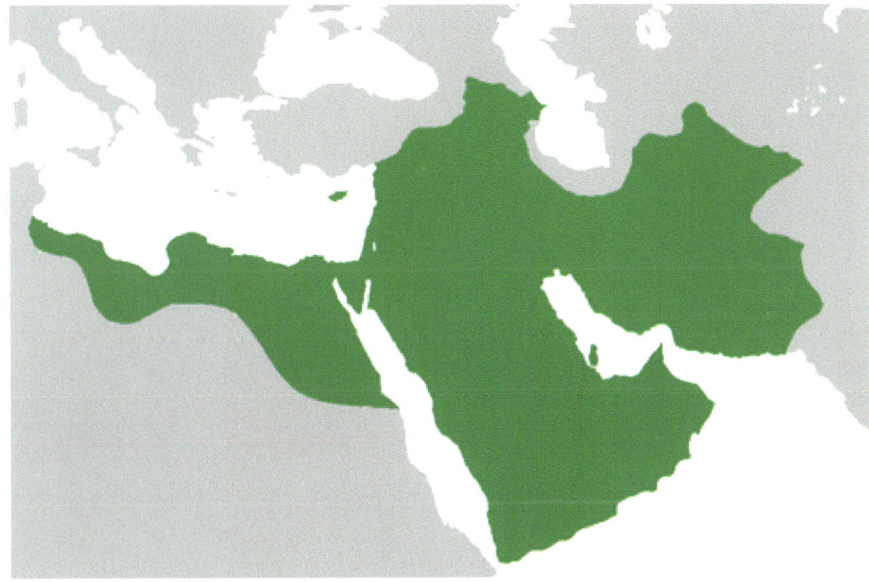

The Rashidun Empire during 'Uthman's khalifah

While the Rashidun Empire had expanded in every direction, most of the inhabitants of the conquered lands had accepted Islam. Those who had chosen to keep their religion were treated justly and mercifully. 'Uthman* commanded that the conquests should go beyond any rebellious areas taking borders much farther out so that there would remain no far-off regions of the Muslim empire which could easily rebel whenever they liked. He personally chose the leaders of armies that would undertake those tasks. Surprisingly, none of them lost a single battle, excluding only one.

Troubles Are Coming

LOSING THE RING

Everything was going well in the khalifah of 'Uthman until the day he lost the ring of the Prophet ﷺ.

Prophet Muhammad ﷺ had a ring engraved with 'Muhammad Rasulallah', which he used to seal letters by pressing it into hot wax. The ring passed to Abu Bakr and then to 'Umar and now to 'Uthman. 'Uthman was at a well one day and the ring slipped off his finger and dropped into the well. Try as he might, he could not find it even though he drained it. He was very distressed. He then made a duplicate ring.

But things seemed to change after this event. In 654 'Uthman began to receive complaints from the various provinces that the governors were oppressing them with harsh treatment and the stipends or payments set by Khalifah 'Umar were too high. There were also other criticisms of 'Uthman himself: that he employed too many of his own family in important positions and that 'Uthman was too old, as he was then in his eighties, to lead properly.

IRAQ

In Kufa and Basra in Iraq, there was a policy about grazing animals. Iraqis were told they could not graze their animals on public lands to make room for huge amounts of camels. They thought these were 'Uthman's although, in fact, they were for the army and charity. Unfortunately, 'Uthman was not told about this.

Sayyidina 'Umar had appointed Amar ibn Yasir, one of the earliest followers of Islam, as the governor of Kufa. Amar ibn Yasir was a son of slaves who had all, as a family, endured unspeakable torture. His parents were killed in front of him and the Quraysh were pressing him to renounce his religion. He finally said the words they wanted to hear and was released. He went straight to the Prophet ﷺ who advised him that was the best thing to do and became one of his most devoted followers.

When 'Uthman came to be khalifa, Amar disagreed with some of 'Uthman's policies but was generally in agreement. But when Amar arrived from Kufa for the first meeting of the governors and went to see 'Uthman, 'Uthman was unavailable and told his servant to tell Amar that he was busy and to wait. Amar was not happy about this and argued with the servant. Then they got in a fight and the servant began to beat him.

Unfortunately, 'Uthman again did not know what happened and was not informed.

EGYPT

IBN ABI SA'HR

In Egypt, Ibn Abi Sa'hr had been appointed: he was the cousin of Uthman. He had replaced 'Amr ibn al-'As who had been a popular and well-liked governor and military general.

Ibn Abi Sa'hr had initially accepted Islam but then changed his mind, acting as a spy temporarily for the Quraysh and then accepted Islam again. He was pardoned by the Prophet ﷺ but his deeds were remembered.

He was paranoid and cruel to those who opposed him. He also wasted huge amounts of money. Messages were sent to 'Uthman to remove him but they had no response - 'Uthman may not have received them - and this led to more unrest.

MUHAMMAD BIN ABU BAKR

In Egypt, the anti-'Uthman group was continuing to grow under the leadership of Muhammad ibn Abi Bakr. Muhammad ibn Abi Bakr's sister was 'Aisha. He was two years old when his father Abu Bakr died. His mother then married 'Ali ibn Talib so he grew up in 'Ali's house and believed that 'Ali should be Khalifa and that 'Uthman should abdicate in his favour.

THE SECOND MEETING BEFORE HAJJ

The bad feeling was still increasing, especially in Egypt, so 'Uthman* summoned the governor, 'Abdullah ibn Saad, to Medina to have a meeting about what should be done. 'Abdullah ibn Saad came to Medina, leaving the affairs of Egypt to his deputy, Muhammad ibn Abi Hudhayfah, but when he was away, Muhammad staged a coup d'état and took power.

On hearing of the revolt in Egypt, 'Abdullah hastened back, but 'Uthman* was not in a position to offer him any military assistance, so 'Abdullah was unable to suppress the revolt. Egypt was now in the hands of the rebel group.

In 655, 'Uthman* directed those with any grievance against the government, as well as all the governors throughout the khalifah, to assemble at Makkah for the Hajj, promising that all legitimate grievances would be heard.

The assembly took place in a small village outside Makkah, where large crowds of people from as far away as Kufa, Egypt and Basra and all the governors gathered.

Arab Street Scene, 20th century

'Abdullah ibn Saad, the other governor of Egypt was worried about these events and began to report to 'Uthman* about the opposition's activities.

FIRST MEETING - THE MAJLIS AL-SHURAH

'Uthman* called all twelve governors from the various provinces to Medina to discuss the problems at the Majlis al-Shurah (council of ministers). After receiving various reports, they tried to decide what should be done with all the rebels. Different ideas were suggested such as sending them to the front lines to keep them occupied, give them money, exile them from the provinces, set an example by whipping the ring leaders or simply to kill them all.

'Uthman* did not want to take any drastic action and agreed to send agents to each area to find out what was going on. 'Uthman* then sent Muhammad ibn Maslamah to Kufa, Usama ibn Zayd to Basra, 'Abdullah ibn Umar to Syria and Amar ibn Yasir to Egypt. When Amar ibn Yasir* arrived in Egypt, the beating he received from 'Uthman's* servant still fresh in his mind, he decided to stay and join the rebellion.

The agents sent to Kufa, Basra and Syria reported that all was well - the people were generally satisfied with the administration, although some individuals had minor personal grievances.

They concluded they would have another meeting a year later.

A shurah is a meeting to decide matters of the community.

REBELS IN MEDINA

Among these crowds were contingents from the various provinces with possible instructions to assassinate 'Uthman and overthrow the government.

Before the meeting, representatives of the Egyptian contingent went to 'Ali ، offered him their allegiance and asked him to be khalifa, but he turned them down.

Representatives of the contingent from Kufa went to Al-Zubayr and those from Basra went to Talhah, each offering them their allegiance as the next khalifah, but both were similarly turned down. The rebels realised that 'Uthman had more support than they thought amongst the other Sahaabah in Medina and they were not inclined to listen to them. Even though there were several leading Sahaabah who were calling upon 'Uthman to step down, none of them were interested in joining a khwajirite, or rebellious group.

With the large crowds outside, 'Uthman asked for all complaints to be brought forward. He was surprised when they did not complain about the governors but instead started to complain about him. That he gave away wealth and land, high positions to unworthy people and those from his own family. That he blocked public lands for grazing. That he allowed the beating of 'Amr ibn Yasir and that he did not participate in the battle Badr and Uhud.

'Uthman explained that any gifts were from his wealth, and some appointments were from his family, others were not. That 'Amr ibn Yasir's beating was a misunderstanding. He explained that at Badr, he was with his wife, the Prophet's ﷺ daughter, who lay dying and that Allah had forgiven all those who fled at the battle of Uhud.

'Uthman asked what their demands were and they replied that they wished for;

1. A raise in their stipends.

2. Wanted their imprisoned friends released and exiled rather than imprisoned.

3. 'Amr ibn al-'As to be reinstated in Egypt.

'Uthman agreed and the people were content and went off to begin the Hajj.

It is said that before returning to Syria, the governor Mu'awiyah, 'Uthman's cousin, suggested that 'Uthman should come with him to Syria as the atmosphere there was peaceful, just in case there was any more trouble, but 'Uthman rejected his offer, saying that he didn't want to leave the city of Muhammad ﷺ. Mu'awiyah then suggested that he be allowed to send a strong force from Syria to Medina to guard 'Uthman against any possible attempt by rebels to harm him. 'Uthman rejected it too, saying that the Syrian forces in Medina would be an incitement to civil war, and he could not agree to that.

'Amr Ibn al-'As Mosque in Fustat, Egypt.

Arabs Planning a Revolt by HM Burton

THE MESSAGE

All seemed fairly settled until a messenger was caught leaving Medina with a note that had been stamped with the seal of the Prophet ﷺ, supposedly from 'Uthman. This note was addressed to the governor of Egypt instructing them to punish the rebellious group returning from Medina in any way they liked. It seemed as if 'Uthman was recommending harsh treatment of the rebels, even though an agreement had been reached. But this note could not have been written or authorised by 'Uthman as it was opposite to his nature. (Later it was discovered that the letter had been written by Marwan ibn al-Hakam.)

The people became furious and soon an armed group, mainly Egyptians, arrived in Medina and were met by 'Ali ibn Abi Talib himself at the outskirts, who explained the gravity of the error and the falsehood of the rumours to them. The plea fell on deaf ears, and they went ahead to confront 'Uthman and put his household under a long siege. His advisors said he needed to take action quickly, either send for the army or move to a safer place or have guards protecting his house. Because of his honesty and forthright personality, he did not use the funds from the treasury to employ additional guards for himself and his home.

'Ali ibn Abi Talib sent his sons Hasan and Husayn along with several others to defend 'Uthman, but they refused to fight the rebels for fear of causing the death of Muslims. There were also very few men in Medina, as many were still in Makkah for the Hajj or far off on one of the fronts.

The rebels surrounded his house, shouting at him to abdicate.

'Uthman appealed to their reason. He told them he knew nothing about the letter. They would shout out verses of the Qur'an and 'Uthman told them that he was there when they were revealed and they were taking them completely out of context.

He did not want to kill the rebels as he hated the idea of Muslims killing Muslims.

He replied, "By Allah, I would not be the first successor of the Messenger of Allah ﷺ to lead his nation to bloodshed …I would not depart from the homeland of my migration, or the neighbourhood of the Messenger of Allah ﷺ as long as I am living."

Muslim ibn Sa'eed, a freed slave of 'Uthman, reported that one day during the long siege, 'Uthman freed twenty slaves.

After this 'Uthman said, "I saw the Messenger of Allah ﷺ in a dream, as well as Abu Bakr and 'Umar, and they said to me, 'Be patient, for you are going to break your fast with us soon.'" Another version states that he said: "The Prophet ﷺ asked me, 'Shall we send forces to defeat the rebels or do you prefer to join us today for fast breaking?' To which I replied that I prefer to join them." Then he requested a copy of the Qur'an and he opened it in front of him and made the intention to fast that day.

The Martyrdom of 'Uthman

'Uthman ordered his companions to leave and only his wife Nayla was with him. The Egyptian rebels then broke into 'Uthman's house. Muhammad ibn Abu Bakr entered with the others. 'Uthman said to him, "Your father would not be pleased with this!" Muhammad then seemed to come to his senses and left the house.

The others grouped around 'Uthman, taunting him, swords at the ready. Nayla threw herself in front of 'Uthman to protect him and raised her hand to deflect a sword. She had the end of her fingers chopped off and was pushed aside. The assassin's sword then struck 'Uthman while the Qur'an was still in his hand, and in more than one report, the first drop of his blood fell upon the words

"Verily, Allah sufficeth thee; He is the All-Hearing, the All-Knowing." [Qur'an 2:137]

Ibn Asakir reported that when 'Uthman received the first blow, he said, *"Bismillah, tawakkaltu 'ala Allah"* (In the name of Allah, and upon Allah I do rely on). When his blood poured forth, he said, *"SubhaanAllah al-'Adhim"* (Glory be to Allah, the Majestic).

They then dealt the final blow to his head. 'Uthman breathed his last breath on Friday afternoon, 17 Dhul-Hijjah, 656 (35 A.H.)

The grave of Sayyidina 'Uthman

FUNERAL

His friends and family left 'Uthmans body in his house for two days for fear of being assaulted when they left the house and quietly brought the body to the Jewish cemetery, a little way from the Muslim graveyard so that his body would not be disturbed. As he was a martyr, his body was not washed nor was it given a burial shroud.

He was buried by Hasan, Husayn, 'Ali and others. Nayla followed the funeral with a lamp, but, to maintain secrecy, the lamp had to be extinguished. Nayla was accompanied by some women, including 'Uthman's daughter.

For three days chaos ruled in Medina, and wild gangs roamed the city. People shut themselves in their homes.

Some decades later, the Umayyad rulers demolished the wall separating the two cemeteries and merged the Jewish cemetery into the Muslim one to ensure that his tomb was now inside a Muslim cemetery.

The rebels looted the house, even snatching the women's veils. Wanting to find hidden wealth, they opened his cabinet and found a box in which there was a note that read:

"This is the testament of 'Uthman before Allah: In the name of Allah, the Most Gracious, the Most Merciful. 'Uthman bin Affan bears witness that there is no true deity but Allah and that Muhammad is Allah's Messenger. Paradise is true and Hell is true, and Allah will resurrect everyone on the Day of Judgment, for Allah will never break His Promise."

The rebels left the house as the supporters of 'Uthman arrived at the gate, but it was too late. The rebels fled and could not be found by the Companions.

WHAT LED TO 'UTHMAN'S MARTYRDOM?

The martydom of 'Uthman ibn Affan, may Allah be well pleased with him, was predicted by the Prophet ﷺ, as were the rebellions. The Prophet ﷺ said, "A dissention shall surge like so many bull's horns. At that time, he (pointing to a man with a veil) and whoever is with him are on the side of right." Ka'b b. Murra al-Bhazi ran up to him and lifted the veil and turned him towards the Prophet ﷺ and said, "Him, Messenger of Allah?" The Prophet ﷺ said, "Yes." It was 'Uthman ibn Affan.

If we look back at his Khalifah, 'Uthman assumed this role at a relatively old age. Being a pious and gentle man but also very diplomatic, he was able to govern wisely and kindly. He loved the Qur'an and would spend a lot of time reading it with his wife Nayla, as well as attending to matters of state and being the religious leader of the Muslims.

However, the Empire was expanding at a huge rate, as a young and powerful new religion reaching far lands. 'Umar al-Khattab before him was highly vigilant; his warrior nature and fierce love of justice did not let oppression develop; personally travelling to far-off lands or immediately summoning governors or generals if he heard of any behaviour that was not just.

'Uthman perhaps lacked that extra energy needed for quick and decisive action when dissension grew. He overlooked grievances and did not act swiftly. Governors probably grew aware that 'Uthman was not going to come down hard on them, so authoritarianism developed and oppression grew. 'Uthman's decision to appoint many of his family members initially was a positive move, for better communication and loyalty, but he was accused of nepotism (preferring his own family for positions of power).

Losing the ring down a well halfway through his khalifate seemed to bring an end to the blessed leadership as things deteriorated after this event.

But what makes 'Uthman stand out, besides being one of the very first Muslims, being beloved to the Prophet ﷺ as well as his endless generosity, was that 'Uthman did not want to shed the blood of one Muslim, even a rebellious and misguided one, to save his own life.

Most, or shall we say probably the majority of people in power, would not think twice about having armed guards to protect them, dealing harshly with those against them, or hide in a secret bunker.

Sayyidina 'Uthman however chose not to resort to any of these actions. 'Uthman did not fear death, and indeed looked forward to breaking his fast with the Holy Prophet ﷺ and Abu Bakr and 'Umar, as foretold in his dream the night before. The world, the power he had, meant nothing, compared to the endless bliss of the company of those beloved to him.

He freed twenty slaves on the morning of his departure to the next life and instructed his companions to leave the house so they would not have to fight other Muslims. His devoted wife Nayla refused to leave his side and so they read Qur'an together until the rebels entered the house. Sayydina 'Uthman left this world with the Qur'an in his hand, Tawheed on his tongue, a blessed and pure soul.

May Allah bless Sayyidina 'Uthman, of whom the Prophet ﷺ said, *"Every prophet has a companion in Paradise and mine is 'Uthman."*

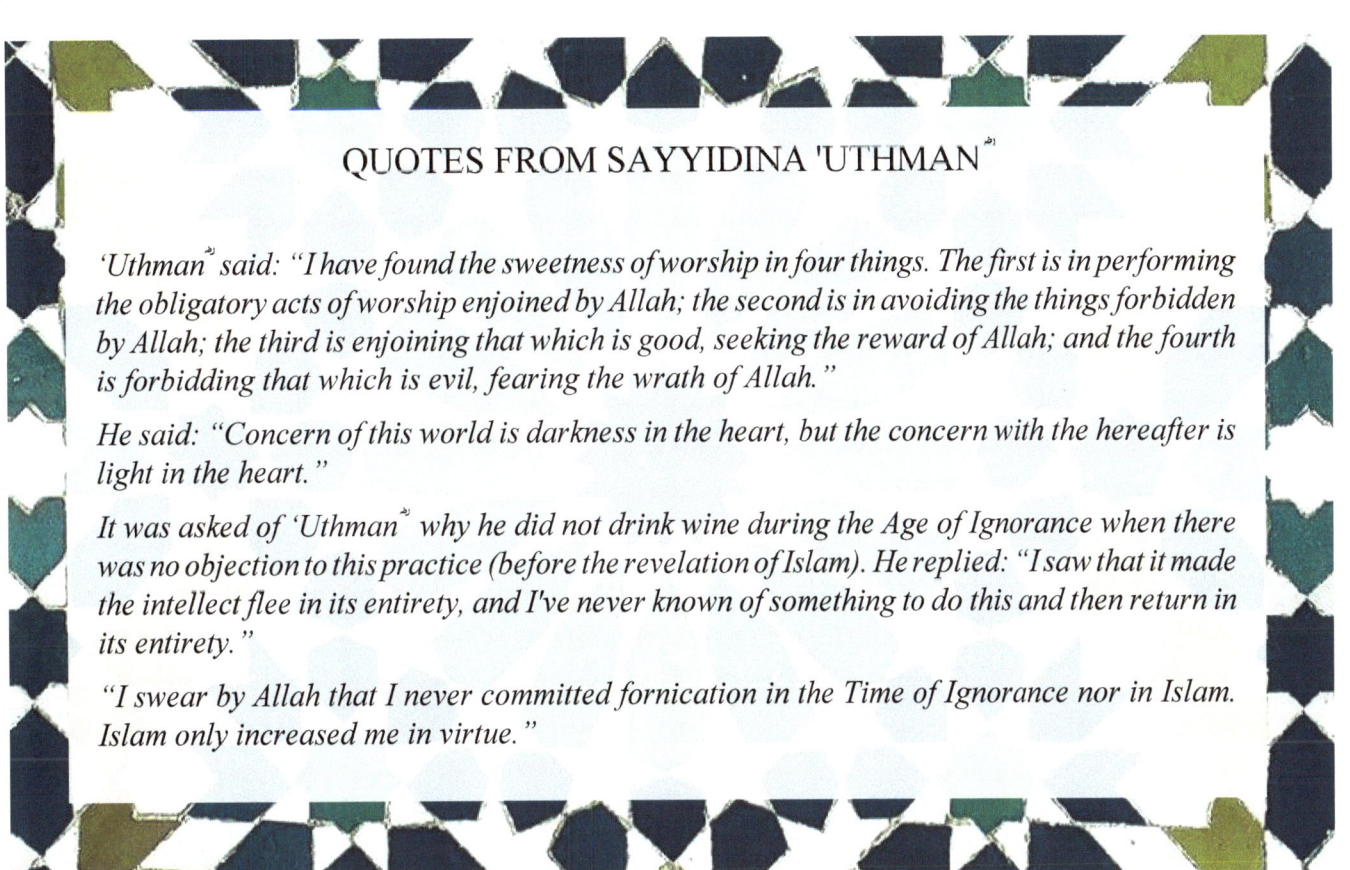

QUOTES FROM SAYYIDINA 'UTHMAN

'Uthman said: *"I have found the sweetness of worship in four things. The first is in performing the obligatory acts of worship enjoined by Allah; the second is in avoiding the things forbidden by Allah; the third is enjoining that which is good, seeking the reward of Allah; and the fourth is forbidding that which is evil, fearing the wrath of Allah."*

He said: *"Concern of this world is darkness in the heart, but the concern with the hereafter is light in the heart."*

It was asked of 'Uthman why he did not drink wine during the Age of Ignorance when there was no objection to this practice (before the revelation of Islam). He replied: *"I saw that it made the intellect flee in its entirety, and I've never known of something to do this and then return in its entirety."*

"I swear by Allah that I never committed fornication in the Time of Ignorance nor in Islam. Islam only increased me in virtue."

'Ali ibn Abi Talib ⌖

One of the most beloved Companions of the Prophet ﷺ, and the cousin of the Prophet ﷺ. He was one of the first to accept Islam and was the first child to accept Islam. He was a devoted Companion of the Prophet ﷺ, the husband of Fatima, the daughter of the Prophet ﷺ.

The Prophet ﷺ said,

"I am the city of knowledge and 'Ali is the gate."

When the verse was revealed: "Come! We will summon our sons and your sons, and our women and your women, and ourselves and yourselves, then we will pray humbly and invoke the curse of Allah upon those who lie"(3:61), the Prophet ﷺ summoned 'Ali, Fatima, Hasan, and Husayn, and said: "O Allah! These are my Family."

The Prophet ﷺ said: "Anyone whose protecting friend (mawla) I am, 'Ali is his protecting friend." 'Umar said: "Congratulations, O 'Ali! You have become the protecting friend of every single believer."

The Prophet ﷺ said: " 'Ali is part of me and I am part of 'Ali! No-one conveys something on my behalf except I or he." (The context of this hadith was the conveyance of Sura Bara'a to the Quraysh and the rescinding of the Prophet's ﷺ pact with them.)

When the Prophet ﷺ sent 'Ali to Yemen the latter said: "O Messenger of Allah, you are sending me to people who are older than me so that I judge between them!" The Prophet ﷺ said: "Go, for verily Allah shall empower your tongue and guide your heart." 'Ali said: "After that I never felt doubt as to what judgement I should pass between two parties."

'Umar said: "'Ali is the best in judgement among us, and Ubayy is the most proficient at the Qur'anic readings." Ibn Mas'ud similarly said: "We used to say that the best in judgement among the people of Medina was 'Ali."

'Ali's Upbringing

When Muhammad ﷺ was orphaned, and after his grandfather died, 'Ali's father, Abu Talib ibn Abd al-Muttalib, took Muhammad into his house, and raised him as one of his own. Abu Talib was the custodian of the Ka'aba.

Many years later, 'Ali ibn Abi Talib was born on the 13th of September 601. Some reports say he was born in the holy house of the Ka'aba. 'Ali shared the same lineage as the Prophet Muhammad ﷺ, being descended from the Prophet Ismael.

Muhammad ﷺ married Khadija and a few years later, they invited 'Ali to come and live at their house, so 'Ali grew up in the blessed house of the Prophet ﷺ.

'Ali was devoted to the Prophet ﷺ and stood up and agreed with him, when even his own family rejected him.

"Not a single verse of the Qur'an (was revealed to) the Messenger of God which he did not proceed to dictate to me and he would instruct me as to its tafsir (the literal explanation) and the (the spiritual exegesis), the verse which abrogates, and the abrogated verse, and the fixed and the ambiguous, the particular and the general ...[166]"

One day, at age nine or ten, 'Ali found the Prophet ﷺ and Khadija praying. He asked about it and the Prophet ﷺ told him about the visitation of the Angel Jibreel in the cave of Hira and that Allah has asked them to tell people to not worship idols. He immediately accepted the Message.

'ALI ﺀ AS A SCRIBE

It was 'Ali ﺀ who was given the task, along with other scribes, to write down the Qur'an as it was revealed. He was also given the task to scribe the Treaty of Hudaybiyah.

When negotiating with the Makkans, they wanted 'Ali to delete the phrase "Messenger of Allah" under the name of the Prophet ﷺ. They said, "If we believed that then there wouldn't be any problems." The Prophet ﷺ indicated for 'Ali to cross out this phrase. 'Ali wanted to obey the Prophet ﷺ but such was his love and respect, he couldn't bring himself to cross out those blessed words of truth. The Prophet ﷺ himself then asked 'Ali to point out where it was written, and with his own blessed hands crossed out the phrase.

Parchment leaf from a copy of the Quran written in early Kufic script, Syria, early 8th century in AH 75 (694), The David Collection, Copenhagen

A band of assassins, each from a different tribe, failed to kill the Prophet ﷺ as 'Ali lay there instead. Painting by Hassan Roholamin.

THE STORY OF 'ALI'S ﺀ BRAVERY

When 'Ali ﺀ was around 22 or 23 years old, the Prophet ﷺ received the Divine Order to immediately migrate to Medina, he prepared to go and asked Abu Bakr ﺀ, his best friend to accompany him.

He asked 'Ali ﺀ to sleep in his bed instead of him that night. He knew that there was an evil plot to kill him in the night and that they would not slay 'Ali ﺀ. 'Ali ﺀ bravely and immediately said yes, and went to bed in the Prophet's ﷺ bed so that the assassins would think the Prophet ﷺ was there.

The Quraysh were already gathering but the Prophet ﷺ slipped out undetected because he recited the first ten verses of Surah Ya Seen which made him invisible to the Quraysh.

Later that night, the Quraysh crept into the house of the Prophet ﷺ and were about to strike the man sleeping in the bed until one man cried out, "That's not Muhammad!" They uncovered the figure and it was 'Ali ﺀ.

Ali﷿ and Fatima﷿

THEIR MARRIAGE

"When Allah ordered the Prophet ﷺ to find a husband for his daughter, the Prophet ﷺ called all the Companions without discrimination and said to them, "God has ordered me to say that whoever recites the Quran from beginning to end tonight may marry my daughter, Fatima if she consents."

That night, all the Companions tried to recite the Quran from beginning to end. All stayed at the mosque trying to finish except 'Ali ibn Abi Talib﷿, who went home and slept. Everyone, including the blessed Prophet ﷺ, assembled in the mosque when Bilal recited the call for the dawn prayer. After performing the dawn prayer, Prophet Muhammad ﷺ asked, "Who finished the Quran last night so that I can marry him to my daughter Fatima?" No one was able to answer, because it is very difficult to finish the thirty parts of the Quran in only seven or eight hours.

'Ali ibn Abi Talib﷿ said, "O Messenger of God, I finished reciting the Quran last night."

The other Companions looked at him and said, "How is it that you finished the Quran? You slept all night."

He said, "No, I completed Quran from beginning to end."

The Prophet ﷺ said to 'Ali﷿, "Who is your witness?"

'Ali﷿ said, "God is my witness and you, O Prophet ﷺ, are my witness that I completed it. O Messenger of God, I recited the following: 'There is no god but God, Muhammad is the Messenger of God' three times; 'I seek the forgiveness of God' seventy times; the Opening Chapter once; the Chapter of Sincerity three times; the Chapter of the Dawn once; then the Chapter of Humanity once; 'There is no god but God' ten times; and, ten times 'Peace and the blessings of God be upon Muhammad and his family.'"

The Prophet ﷺ said, "As God bears witness, I also bear witness that Ali has completed the Quran. If you recite what he recited, it is equivalent to having completed the Quran."

The Prophet ﷺ asked Fatima, "O Fatima, do you accept 'Ali as your husband?"

She said, "On one condition."

All the Companions looked at 'Ali﷿, at Fatima﷿, and the Prophet ﷺ. The Prophet's ﷺ face changed as he wondered why Fatima said this? What could the condition be? The angel Gabriel عليهوسلم came and told him, "O Prophet, do not make a quick decision concerning her. God is telling you to ask her what her condition is."

The Prophet ﷺ said, "O Fatima, what is your condition?"

She said, "The condition does not concern 'Ali, but it is related to me. If that condition is fulfilled, I will accept. If not, I will never accept to marry 'Ali."

Again, the angel Gabriel عليهوسلم came to the Prophet saying, "God is ordering you to ask her what her condition is." Now, look at what God had put into her heart and consider the benefit and station of women in spirituality.

The Prophet ﷺ said, "O Fatima, what is your condition?"

She said, "I hear you continuously, day and night, praying for your Community. You say, 'O my Lord! Permit me to lead my Community to you! Forgive them! Purify them! Take away their sins and difficulties and burdens!' I hear you and know how much you suffer for your Community. I know from what you have said that when you pass away, you will still be saying, 'My Community!' before your Lord, in your grave, and on Judgment Day. My father, I see you suffering so much for your Community. Since that love of your Community is also in my heart, I want your Community as my dowry. If you accept, I will marry Ali."

She asked for all of the Prophet's Community, everyone without discrimination. What was the Prophet ﷺ going to say? It was not in his hand to give such a dowry. He waited for Gabriel (as), but Gabriel did not come quickly. He kept him waiting for some time, then came and said, "God sends you His greetings and accepts Fatima's request. He gives her what she asked for as her dowry to marry 'Ali." The Prophet ﷺ immediately stood up and performed two rak`ats of prostrations of thankfulness to his Lord.

Fatima﷿ was only concerned with the salvation of the Community of the Prophet ﷺ. No one is going to be outside of her dowry because if God removes one person from the dowry, it will be as if her marriage to 'Ali﷿ had been invalid. Therefore, she is going to take the entire Community under her wing and they shall enter with her into Paradise. This is from the power of one Muslim woman. She will take everyone with her into Paradise.

What about other such women in Islam? What will their power be? What about saints? What about prophets? God has created human beings pure. He keeps them pure with such power as that of the Prophet ﷺ, Abu Bakr﷿, 'Umar﷿, 'Uthman﷿, 'Ali﷿, and especially our grandmother, Fatima al-Zahrah﷿, as well as our Grandshaykh, our shaykh, and the masters of the Naqshbandi Order and other orders. May God guide us and all seekers in the Way of Divine Love and the Divine Presence."

From Naqshbandi Sufi Way by Sheikh Hisham Kabbani

FATIMA'S REQUEST

Fatima came to the Prophet ﷺ asking for a servant. He said, "May I inform you of something better than that? When you go to bed, recite 'SubhaanAllah' thirty three times, 'Alhamdulillah' thirty three times, and Allahu Akbar thirty four times.' ''Ali added, I have never failed to recite it ever since.' Somebody asked, 'Even on the night of the battle of Siffin?' He said, 'Even on the night of the battle of Siffin.'" (Narrated by 'Ali.)

THE STORY OF THE POMEGRANATE

'Ali entered the house and gave his greetings to his wife, Fatima, the most beloved daughter of the Prophet ﷺ. She had a pain in her stomach and requested 'Ali to take the few dirhams she had to buy some pomegranates for her. 'Ali ibn Abi Talib obliged and purchased a pomegranate from the market. On the way home, a poor man in the street waved to him, saying "Yaa 'Ali, I'm a very poor man. Do you know what I want? I want a pomegranate." Without any hesitation 'Ali immediately gave the poor man the pomegranate, explaining that he had bought it for his wife but gave it to the poor man instead for the sake of Allah. The poor man offered to take half the pomegranate only, but 'Ali refused and instead went home empty-handed. He explained the incident to Fatima when he got home. Immediately, she replied, "Best, what you did. It is better that you give it to the poor person." Sometime later, there was a knock on the door. It was Salman al-Farsi bearing a tray of nine pomegranates in his hand. He said that a man had come to the Prophet ﷺ, asking him to give the pomegranates to 'Ali. 'Ali enquired whether this was all that the Prophet ﷺ gave him. Salman al-Farsi revealed that there was a tenth pomegranate that he had purposely concealed! After a while, 'Ali enquired with the Prophet ﷺ what had transpired. Rasoolullah ﷺ replied that the poor man was Angel Jibreel عليهوسلم, who, in the form of a man, had come to check 'Ali's *iman*. After 'Ali passed the test, Allah sent down the ten pomegranates for the obedience and sacrifice of 'Ali and his wife for the path of Allah – for Allah rewards tenfold for every good deed performed.

'Ali's Military Career

'Ali took part in almost all the battles during the time of the Prophet ﷺ. The exception was the battle of Tabuk, when the Prophet specifically asked 'Ali to remain behind. 'Ali pleaded; "O Messenger of Allah! Are you leaving me behind with the women and children?" The Prophet ﷺ replied: "Are you not happy to stand next to me like Harun next to Musa, save that there is no Prophet after me?"

In the battle of Badr, at a young age, 'Ali stood out as a fearless and skilled warrior, not only defeating the Qurayshi champion, Walid ibn 'Utba, but won every duel he took part in.

He commanded the Muslim army in the Battle of the Trench, where he defeated the legendary Arab warrior 'Amr ibn 'Abd al-Wud. Muhammad ﷺ made 'Ali commander at this battle, claiming, "I will hand the standard to a man who loves Allah and His Messenger and is loved by Allah and His Messenger. He will come back with conquest."

After this battle, the Prophet ﷺ gave 'Ali the name Asadullāh (which means 'Lion of God'), which follows the surname his mother gave him of 'Haydar' which means 'Lion'.

He was also the standard bearer in most of the battles. In the battle of Khaybar, the Prophet ﷺ said, "I would certainly give this standard to a person who loves Allah and his Messenger, and Allah and his Messenger love him too."

'Ali recited this verse on the battle field at Khaybar, *"I'm he whose mother called Haydarah! Like the beast of jungles awesome to see!"*

'Ali was given the famous sword, Zulfiqar by the Prophet ﷺ. 'Ali used it so effectively that a famous known saying emerged: "There is no hero and man like 'Ali - there is no sword like Zulfiqar." the original no longer exists but it is said to have been scissor-like as this flag depicts.

LIFE AFTER THE PROPHET LEFT THIS WORLD

Not long after the Prophet ﷺ died, 'Ali's beloved wife Fatima, the Prophet's ﷺ daughter also passed to the next life, much to his great sorrow. Over the next 24 years, 'Ali did not take part in any battle or take a role of power. He preferred to have the life of a farmer and to tend the lands around Medina. He dug lots of wells and gave them as gifts to the people. These are known today as 'Ali's wells.' He also assisted Sayyidina 'Umar as an advisor and a judge and became the chief judge of Medina.

Illustration of an Islamic Judge in court. 17th century

'Ali as Khalifah

After the assassination of 'Uthman, the Companions sought out 'Ali to assume the khalifat. 'Ali was reluctant to assume the khalifate, but so many of the older Companions insisted. There is some uncertainty as to who initially voluntarily offered allegiance to 'Ali, but almost unanimously, the people of Medina all gave their allegiance, delighted that 'Ali was chosen, however, there were some that were not pleased with the decision, notably the clan of the Umayyads, of which 'Uthman had been chief.

'Ali then made a speech to the people of Medina when he assumed khalifa, stating that the Muslims were divided and there was unrest everywhere. He reminded people to live according to the ways of the Prophet ﷺ and warned that he would deal harshly with those wishing to cause problems.

INITIAL ACTIONS

'Ali moved to Kufa in Iraq to govern from there after he became the khalifah in order to manage the military frontiers more efficiently.

One of the first things 'Ali did, was to immediately remove the governors who were known for their corruption and injustice. Some in Medina were concerned that this may not have been the best way to go about it, as there was not time to find replacements but 'Ali refused to be complicit in any further injustice. All of the governors accepted 'Ali's decision, except Mu'awiya of the Umayyad clan in Syria.

On instructing the new governor of Egypt, Malik al-Ashtar, 'Ali said, "Let the dearest of treasuries be the treasury of righteous action…Infuse your heart with mercy, love and kindness for your subjects. Be not in the face of them, a voracious animal, counting them as easy prey, for they are of two kinds: Either your brothers in religion or your equals in Creation."

In another letter to Malik al-Ashtar, 'Ali said, "Remember that displeasure and disapproval of common men, have-nots and depressed persons more than outweighs the approval of important persons. The displeasure of a few 'important' people will be excused by the Lord if the general public and masses of your subjects are happy with you. The common men, the poor, apparently less important sections of your subjects are the pillars of Islam….be more friendly with them and secure their confidence and sympathy."

WHAT WAS SAYYIDINA 'ALI* LIKE?

As he grew older, 'Ali* was described as having white hair which he parted in the middle, a very large white beard, and large, heavy eyes. He was heavyset and his height was medium to short.

'Ali* did not care for the luxurious of the world. When Ibn al-Nabbah came to him with the news that the treasury-house was filled with gold and silver 'Ali* summoned the people of Kufa and distributed everything to them with the words: "O Yellow, O White! Go fool other than me." Then he ordered the treasury-house swept, and he prayed two rak`a in it.

Jurmuz said: "I saw 'Ali coming out of his palace wearing a waist-cloth that reached to the middle of his shank and an outer garment tucked up at the sleeves, walking in the marketplace while hitting a small drum (dirra) and enjoining upon people Godwariness and honesty in transactions."

Arabic calligraphy means "There is no brave youth except 'Ali and there is no sword which renders service except Dhul-Fiqar."

REBELLION AND DISCONTENT

Widespread discontent was brewing. Many people felt that 'Ali* did not make enough effort to find the killers of 'Uthman*, including Sayyidinata 'Aisha*. Mu'awiya, the governor of Syria, was enraged that the killing was not yet avenged and blamed 'Ali* for being complacent. Arab traditions were strong and failing to avenge the assassination of so great a man as 'Uthman* was unheard of. 'Ali* had tried all he could to find them, but due to unrest in the provinces, he was unable to get the help that he needed from the people there.

There was also much suspicion because the rebels who attacked 'Uthman* happened to be supporters of 'Ali*. Even though 'Ali* was not part of their plotting, 'Ali had voiced his disapproval of 'Uthman's generous gifts to relatives and may have had other reservations about 'Uthmans' khalifah.

One day, the two companions, Zubayr* and Talha* went to Makkah to perform Umrah. They found Sayyidinata 'Aisha*, their cousin and the wife of the Prophet ﷺ who was calling on the Muslims themselves to find the killers of 'Uthman* and to depose 'Ali*. They also did not support 'Ali and said they only had sworn allegiance to 'Ali* under duress. It is also thought that Talha* and Zubayr* had ambitions to be governors themselves and were angered to not have been appointed by 'Ali*, and now perhaps also wanted the khalifah for one of themselves. They were joined by others who had allegiance to the Umayyad clan, so Makkah became a hotbed of rebellion against Sayyidina 'Ali*.

WHO WERE ZUBAYR* AND TALHA*?

Zubayr ibn al-Awwam* was one of the first men to accept Islam under the guidance of Abu Bakr and was someone who was promised Paradise by the Prophet Muhammad ﷺ. He was one of the best commanders of the Muslim army in the time of the Prophet Muhammad ﷺ and fought in the Battle of Badr and after the success of the Battle of the Trench, the Prophet ﷺ gave him the title of 'Disciple of the Messenger of Allah'. He was also an army commander during Abu Bakr's and 'Umar's khilafah. During 'Uthman's khalifate, he was one of the chief advisers on both political and religious issues. Zubayr* may have had hopes of becoming the next khalif after 'Uthman died, as he had such a long and successful career.

Talha ibn 'Ubayd Allah al Taymi* was one of the ten Companions who were promised Paradise by the Prophet ﷺ. He took part in the early battles and memorised the Qur'an. Abu Bakr* appointed Talha to lead some battles. He then became a council member for the khalifah

BATTLE OF THE CAMEL

656 C.E. (36 A.H.)

BASRA

Together, with an army of 600-900 from Makkah, 'Aisha, Talha and Zubayr marched to Basra in Iraq, 1300 km away, where reports that the assassins of 'Uthman were hiding. They may have been joined by forces loyal to Mu'awiya, making their army as many as 10,000 according to some reports.

On the way, they tried to gain support for their cause, although they did not find much. Near Basra, at a place called Hawab, 'Aisha became disheartened by the incessant howling of dogs which reminded her of Muhammad's ﷺ ominous warning years before, *"One of you women shall come out riding a heavy-maned red camel, and the dogs of Hawab will bark at her. Many will be killed to her right and to her left, and she shall escape after near death."* (Tabari) Unfortunately, she was dissuaded from any change of plans by Talha and Zubayr.

When they arrived at Basra, the city was divided between those who were for or against 'Ali, although most were loyal to him. On a cold dark night with wind and rain, the rebels raided the town killing many and seizing control. The governor was imprisoned. They then demanded the surrender of those who took part in 'Uthman's assassination and killed 600 men. The remaining residents were infuriated and called for 'Ali to step in.

'Ali was on his way and wanted to stop them but was not able to reach it in time. With an army enlarged by men from Kufa, 'Ali arrived with some six to seven thousand men.

The two armies camped across from each other outside of Basra. 'Ali appealed to 'Aisha's army, reminding them of their oaths and saying of the Prophet Muhammad ﷺ. Many joined his side or simply left, unwilling to fight in a battle between the Prophets' ﷺ widow and his cousin.

A tent was set up between the two armies and according to some traditions, Imam 'Ali and 'Aisha agreed to a peaceful resolution as they had no real intention to fight each other. 'Ali reminded Zubayr of an incident in their childhood when Muhammad ﷺ had predicted that Zubayr would one day unjustly fight 'Ali. Even with this reminder, negotiations were not finalised because 'Aisha's party demanded that 'Ali give up the khalifah and a council should be appointed to elect a new successor, but 'Ali had been officially elected beforehand in Medina so would not agree, perhaps also knowing that a fair council would not be appointed. There are varying reports of how it was ultimately concluded but most agree there was a peaceful conclusion.

However, there was still an atmosphere of unrest, especially in the rebel army. 'Ali had ordered his army to not begin the fighting and told them if there was to be a battle, then do not kill or take any prisoners and only captured weapons and animals could be considered war booty.

In a last-ditch attempt to stop the battle, 'Ali ordered a copy of the Qur'an to be brought between the battle lines but apparently, the holder was shot.

15th century Persian miniature of 'Ali and 'Aisha at the Battle of the Camel

According to some reports, rebels within the armies ignited the fighting by spreading gossip and rumours and other reports say another group of men attacked the two armies, each believing it was the other side. In any case, the battle began and 13,000 were killed including Talha who was reportedly killed by one of his army, Marwan, who believed Talha to be responsible for the assassination of 'Uthman and perhaps that he removed a serious contender of Mu'awiya.

Zubayr left early into the battle, perhaps regretting the fighting but was followed and killed by one of his army for deserting.

'Aisha was led onto the battlefield, riding a red camel, after which the battle is named, in an armoured canopy. She was eventually captured and brought safely to 'Ali. Together with Talha and Zubayr's death, the battle ended. 'Ali was victorious.

'Aisha went to a house in Basra where she was looked after but reprimanded for what she had done and was escorted back to Makkah.

This battle was a great sadness to all the Companions of the Prophet ﷺ and many refused to fight. Muslims were fighting against Muslims, even against the Companions of the Prophet ﷺ.

PUBLIC PARDON AFTER THE BATTLE OF THE CAMEL

'Ali announced a public pardon after the battle. He had earlier forbidden his men from harming the captives, the deserters, and the wounded. The prisoners were set free and their properties were returned to them. To compensate the army, 'Ali used money from the treasury of Basra. This pardon was also extended to high-profile rebels such as Marwan and the sons of 'Uthman, Talha, and Zubayr. 'Ali asked them if he was not the closest to Muhammad ﷺ and the most entitled to leadership after Muhammad's death. He then let them go after they begged for pardon and pledged their allegiance. A different report holds that a still defiant Marwan was let go without pledging his allegiance to 'Ali.

Afterwards 'Aisha was extremely remorseful and did not engage in politics until her death some sixty years later, following a very simple and pious life. Despite what happened, 'Ali still referred to 'Aisha as the 'Beloved of the of the Messenger of Allah.'

Because 'Ali was lenient with the prisoners of war, this gave rise to the khwajrite movement as seen later, who wanted full compensation for fighting.

This was to become known as the first fitna, due to the arguments, confusion, slander and killings and the lies of people who blamed 'Ali, suggesting he was on the side of the rebels.

MU'AWIYA AND THE CLAN OF THE UMAYYADS

16th Century miniature of the Battle of Siffan.

Mu'awiya, 'Uthman's cousin, was the governor of Damascus and Syria and was the major opponent to Ali's khalifah. He had ideas about himself one day being khalifah. He was part of the Umayyad clan and was publicly against Sayyidina 'Ali, harshly criticising the fact that 'Ali had not yet avenged Sayyidina 'Uthman's killers. He even hung 'Uthman's blood-stained shirt in public to increase ill ease and ordered that Sayyidina 'Ali's name be cursed at the prayers in the mosques.

Despite these insulting actions, Mu'awiya was an efficient governor and ran the Syrian provinces well, so the local people supported him and 'Ali advised those who were against Mu'awiya, "People! Do not loathe Mu'awiya's leadership. If you were to loose him, you would see heads parting like colocythns."

BATTLE OF SIFFAN 657 C.E. (37 A.H.)

After 'Ali appointed 'Abd Allah ibn al-'Abbas as governor of Basra, Mu'awiya decided to mobilise an army against 'Ali, justifying it by saying that his people were not in Medina when 'Ali was elected and therefore it was not a fair decision, even though this was impossible to arrange given the short notice. 'Ali responded by moving his armies north and encamped at Siffan for one hundred days while he tried to reason with Mu'awiya. This was unsuccessful and the battle of Siffan commenced, followed by the deadly battle of Laylat al-Harir (the Night of Clamour).

'Ali's army had almost won this battle until Mu'awiya commanded his soldiers to put pages of the Qur'an on the end of their spears, shouting out verses from them to confuse 'Ali's army, which it did, even though 'Ali saw through his plan and tried to warn the soldiers. Few wanted to continue the fight which led to an agreement that the choice of khalifah should be made by Shura (a council.) 'Ali felt he had to go along with this.

'Abd Allah ibn Abbas and Abu Musa were appointed and were to meet in seven months. 'Abd Allah ibn Abbas, on Mu'awiya's side, managed to convince Abu Musa, that both should step down and a new khalifah appointed. This shocked 'Ali and his followers. It also lowered 'Ali to the same status as the rebellious Mu'awiya. Then, in the public meeting, Abu Musa announced the agreement, but then 'Amr declared 'Ali was deposed and said Mu'awiya was now khalifa. Essentially, Abu Musa had been tricked.

'Ali did not accept this as it was against the Qur'an and Sunna. But because he had agreed to the Shura to begin with, this incident lowered his status among the Muslims (except the Companions in Medina) and he found it hard to raise a large enough army after this event.

What 'Ali said about those times.

"The Umayyads' knowledge of me did not restrain them from accusing me, nor did my precedence in accepting Islam keep these ignorant people from blaming me. Allah's admonitions are more eloquent than my tongue. I am the contester against those who break away from Faith and the opposer of those who entertain doubts. Uncertainties should be placed before the Qur'an, the Book of Allah (for clarification). Certainly, people will be recompensed according to what they have in their hearts."

This fitna lasted until the end of 'Ali's khalifah, mostly inflamed by the Umayyads.

'ALI'S JUSTICE

'Ali's shield went missing after the battle of Siffin. He found it with a Christian man and it was instantly recognized by many, because of its distinctive decorations and markings. 'Ali, who was already khalifa at the time, took the man to the judge as per the Islamic ruling instead of simply confiscating the shield. The judge asked the Christian man to respond to the allegation of the Amir al-Mu'minin (the Governor of the Muslims).

The Christian claimed that the shield was his, but also that Amir al-Mu'minin was not a liar. To this, 'Ali replied that the judge had no right to refer to him as the "Amir al-Mu'minin" when he was appearing before the judge as a normal citizen. He went on to say that the Christian man was in the right, because 'Ali had no evidence with him. The judge ruled in favour of the Christian, who took the shield and left.

After taking a few steps, he came back, and said, "I bear witness what I saw now is the justice of Messengers and Prophets. The Amir al-Mu'minin went to the judge to take his rights from me! I bear witness there is no one worthy of worship except Allah, and I bear witness that Muhammad is the Messenger of Allah." After embracing Islam, the man admitted, "The shield is yours. I followed the army, and at a certain time I took it from you." Later on, people bore witness that this man became one of noble character and died as a soldier of Islam at the Al-Nahrawan battle.

A Persian shield, date unknown.

THE KHWAJARITES (DAESH)

The Khwajarites (meaning those who left the straight path) formed a dangerous group of rebels who were initially part of 'Ali's army. Initially they were pious and memorisers of Qur'an but broke away after he accepted the arbitration and formed their own rebel group. Their slogan was, *"Arbitration belongs to Allah alone."* (6:57, 12:40, 12:67).

When this group of extremists became numerous, 'Ali would meet with the leaders and try to bring them to reason using diplomacy and logical argument. Sayyidina 'Ali was known to be extremely eloquent and wise and often successful in helping people to see reason.

In answer to their slogan, "Arbitration belongs to Allah alone", 'Ali said to them: "A word of truth spoken in the way of falsehood!"

He sent them the expert interpreter of the Qur'an among the Companions, Ibn 'Abbas, who recited to them the verses;

"The judge is to be two men among you known for justice" (5:95)

He raised an army of 20,000 and marched to their stronghold. He called out to the people, "Anyone who wants to leave the Khwarjites and join us, then they are welcome and no harm will come to them!" About half of the Khwarjites then left and joined 'Ali's side. The rest took up their arms and fought with Imam 'Ali's army and all were killed except nine of the leaders who escaped. This was the Battle of Nahrawan.

and *"Appoint an arbiter from his folk and an arbiter from her folk"* (4:35)

Ibn Abbas then said: "Allah has thereby entrusted arbitration to men, although if He had wished to decide He would have decided. And is the sanctity of the Community of Muhammad not greater than that of a man and a woman?" Hearing this, four thousand of the Khawarij came back with him.

However, a large group did not return to 'Ali. They also ignored verses that say,

"Obey Allah, obey the Prophet and obey those in authority among you." (An Nisa 4:59)

The Khwarjites numbered over 5000 and claimed a khalifate for themselves, and made plans to kill Sayyidina 'Ali as well as Mu'awiyya in Syria and 'Amr bin al-As in Egypt and take control for themselves. They had little funds for their ambitions so they took to looting passing caravans.

Finally, when one of the caravans was stopped and a Companion of the Prophet ﷺ was questioned as to their devotions, asking them if they were in favour of Abu Bakr and 'Umar and what of 'Ali? When this Companion said he supported 'Ali, they slit his throat and his pregnant wife and the unborn baby. When news got back to 'Ali, he realised that it was clear that they were outwardly rebellious and they would continue to commit more evil acts.

The Prophet ﷺ had predicted that 'Ali would fight the Khawarij with the words: *"In truth there will be, among you, one who shall fight over the interpretation of the Qur'an just as I fought over its revelation."* Abu Bakr and 'Umar asked: *"Am I he?"* The Prophet ﷺ said: *"No, it is the one who is mending the shoes."* He had given his shoes to 'Ali to mend.

EXTREMISTS IN ISLAM

It is interesting to note that from as early as the khalifah of Abu Bakr, there existed small groups of extreme Muslims who claimed they practised Islamic ways, but they were often very rigid in these, while simultaneously holding extreme non-Islamic views. The worst of their views was that they had the 'real' version of Islam and that anyone who did not follow their way was considered an unbeliever and must therefore be killed. This was opposite to the way taught by the Prophet ﷺ, who was lenient, generous and forgiving.

Muslims are enjoined (strongly encouraged) to pray, fast and give charity with endless rewards both in this life and the next, but they are not punished by authorities if they do not do so. It is forbidden in Islam to force people to do beneficial practices or convert them to a religion, no matter how true you think it is or how much benefit they would get.

Battle between Khosroe and Bahram Chubaina, from the poem Layla and Majnun originally by Nizami, 1540

The Martyrdom of Sayyidina 'Ali

The Prophet ﷺ had predicted 'Ali's death as a *shaheed* when he said, *"This shall be dyed red from this..."* as he pointed to 'Ali's beard and head respectively. The Prophet ﷺ also foretold how his martyrdom would occur. Amar bin Yasir reported that the Prophet ﷺ said to 'Ali, *"The most wretched of men are two: the people of Thamud who killed the camel and the one who would strike you over here (i.e. on the head) until your beard is wet with your blood."*

The morning before his attack, which was the same date as the Battle of Badr, 'Ali had a dream where he saw the Prophet ﷺ. 'Ali narrates that he said to the Prophet ﷺ, *"'Messenger of Allah! What crookedness and contention I have found coming from your community!' He replied, 'Supplicate against them.' I said, 'Oh Allah! Substitute them with something that will be better for me, and substitute me with something that will be worse for them.'"* (Ibn Sa'd)

The remaining Khwajarites had joined with others and continued to conspire to assassinate 'Ali, Mu'awiyah and 'Amr bin Al Aas so that they could claim power. One night, one of the conspirators, 'Abdur-Rahman bin Muljam came into the mosque in Kufa and hid in it, aware that 'Ali would be offering his Fajr prayers there in the morning. 'Ali came out of the gateway calling the people to prayer and was faced by two men armed with swords. Ibn Muljam struck him on the head with a poisoned sword and was caught, while the other hit the arch of the gate and fled.

As he was lying wounded, 'Ali said to his son, "Treat the man kindly and give him food and water. If I die, his life is left to justice, and he shall be slain for the deed he had done; but do not mutilate him, for that was forbidden by the Prophet ﷺ. 'Lo! Allah loves not aggressors'."

On Friday, 20 Ramadan, 40 Hijri, 661, 'Ali passed away. He was sixty-three. 'Ali had always asked Allah that he die as a martyr for the cause of Islam and Allah accepted his prayers.

The Khalifah of 'Ali only lasted 5 years.

'Ali did not want his grave to be exhumed and profaned by his enemies. He thus asked to be buried secretly. It was revealed later during the Abbasid kalifah by Ja'far al-Sadiq that the grave was some miles from Kufa, where a sanctuary arose later and the city Najaf was built around it. In other reports, 'Ali's followers tied the latter's body on a white camel and headed north from Kufa. 'Ali was said to have given instructions to bury his body at the spot where the camel would rest. The camel reportedly expired at Balkh and 'Ali was thus buried there. According to Abu Hamid al-Gharnati in the 12th century, nearly four hundred citizens of Balkh had seen in their dreams that Muhammad ﷺ told them that 'Ali was buried in the village. In the 15th century, 'Abd al-Ghafur Lari was believed to have discovered 'Ali's tomb in Balkh.

EXTREME VENERATION OF 'ALI

Under the Safavid Empire, Sayyidina 'Ali's grave became highly venerated, with some Shi'a Muslims attributing divine qualities to him. The Shi'ites differ from the Sunnis in that they believe that 'Ali should have been the first khalifah after the Prophet ﷺ and do not recognise the khilafah of Abu Bakr, 'Umar and 'Uthman.

The innovations of those who bore excessive love and admiration for 'Ali appeared in his own lifetime and he himself fought them in word and deed. To those that claimed that the Prophet ﷺ had appointed him as successor after him he said: "In truth, Allah's Messenger did not appoint any successor" and: "The Prophet was taken from us, then Abu Bakr was made the successor, so he did as the Prophet had done and according to his path until Allah took him from us; then 'Umar was made the successor, so he did as the Prophet had done and according to his path until Allah took him from us." To those that claimed that he deserved the khilafah better than Abu Bakr and 'Umar he said: "The best of this Community after its Prophet are Abu Bakr and 'Umar." To those that either hated him or overly loved him 'Ali said: "Two types of people shall perish concerning me: a hater

Outside the tomb of Imam 'Ali in Iran

who forges lies about me, and a lover who over-praises me." To those that claimed that he or his family possessed other than the Qur'an which all Muslims had he said: "Whoever claims that we have something which we read other than the Qur'an has lied." Finally, when a group of people came to him saying: "You are He, you are our Lord! *(anta Hu anta Rabbuna)*" he had them executed and then ordered the bodies burnt.

"When my prayers are answered I am happy because it was my wish. When my prayers are not answered, I am even happier because that was Allah's wish."

"Be sure that something is waiting for you after much patience, to astonish you to a degree that you forget the bitterness of the pain."

"If you want to know where your heart is, see where your mind wanders."

"The body is purified by water. The nafs (ego) by tears and the soul is purified by love."

"Certainly, Allah did not create you in vain. He did not neglect you. Rather, He has ennobled you with abundant provision. He has earmarked rewards for you. So fear Allah, O servants of Allah, and be diligent in your quest. Be earnest in righteous actions before the arrival of the destroyer of pleasures (death)."

"Goodness does not consist in having much property and children, but in doing many good deeds, increasing your gentle character, and adorning yourself before people with the worship of your Lord."

From Abu Araka: "I have seen a remnant of the Companions of Allah's Messenger. I see no-one that resembles them. By Allah! They used to rise in the morning dishevelled, dust-covered, pale, with something between their eyes like goat's knees, as they had spent the night chanting Allah's Book, turning from their feet to their foreheads. If Allah was mentioned they swayed the way trees sway on a windy day, then their eyes poured out tears until by Allah, they soaked their clothes. By Allah! It is as if folks today sleep in indifference."

"This world lasts for an hour: Spend it in obedience."

"Knowledge leads to wisdom, accordingly the educated man is the wise one; riches diminish by expenditure, while knowledge is increased by dissemination. A wise man needs each day an hour set apart in which to examine his conscience, and measure what he has gained or lost."

"A brother is like gold and a friend is like diamond. If gold cracks you can melt it and make it just like it was before. If a diamond cracks, it can never be like it was before."

"Dislike in yourself what you dislike in others."

"When you get ill do not get nervous about it and try as much as possible to be hopeful."

"Do not let your difficulties fill you with anxiety, after all it is only in the darkest nights that stars shine more brightly."

Hasan and Husayn   *The Grandsons of the Holy Prophet*

The Messenger of Allah said: "Al-Hasan and al-Husayn are the chiefs of the youth of Paradise and Fatima is the chief of their women."

Al-Bara narrates that the Prophet saw Hasan and Husayn, so he said: "O Allah, I love them, so love them."

Anas bin Malik narrates that the Messenger of Allah was asked: "Which of the people of your house are most beloved to you?" He said, "Al-Hasan and al-Husayn." And he used to say to Fatima, "Call my two sons for me." And he would smell them and hug them.

Abu Sa'eed narrates that the Messenger of Allah said: "Al-Hasan and al-Husayn are the leaders of the youth of Paradise."

'Ali ibn Abi Talib narrates: "The Prophet took Hasan and Husayn by the hand and said, 'Whoever loves me and loves these two, and their father and mother, he shall be with me in my level on the Day of Judgement."

Abu Buraydah narrates:

"The Messenger of Allah was delivering a Khutbah to us when al-Hasan and al-Husayn came, wearing red shirts, walking and falling down. So the Messenger of Allah descended from the Minbar and carried them, and placed them in front of him. Then he said: 'Allah spoke the Truth: Indeed, your wealth and your children are a trial. I looked at these two children walking and falling down, and I could not bear patiently anymore until I interrupted my talk and picked them up."

Ya'la bin Murrah narrates that the Messenger of Allah said: "Husayn is from me, and I am from Husayn. May Allah love those who love Husayn."

Usamah ibn Zayd narrated: "I went to the Prophet one night about something I required and he came out with something (I did not know what) under his cloak. When I had finished telling him my business I asked him what he had under his cloak, and when he opened it I saw al-Hasan and al-Husayn on his hips. He then said, 'These are my sons and my daughter's sons. O Allah, I love them, so I beseech Thee to love them and those who love them."

Bukhari narrated from Ibn Abi Na'm: "I have heard the Prophet saying, 'They (Hasan and Husayn) are my two sweet-smelling flowers in this world.'"

Calligraphy in Arabic that translates, 'God' in the centre, then Muhammad, 'Ali, Fatima, Hasan and Husayn.

Imam Hasan and Imam Husayn were the grandsons of the Holy Prophet by his daughter Fatima. They were both very righteous and stood up for truth and justice. Husayn and his followers became a symbol of resistance inspiring future uprisings against oppressors and injustice. Throughout history, many notable personalities, such as Nelson Mandela and Mahatma Gandhi, have been inspired by Husayn's stand against oppression as an example for their own fights against injustice.

They were the first ones in Arabia to be called 'Hasan' and 'Husayn'. Scholars say that Imam Husayn represents the noble soul. Hasan was said to resemble the Prophet Muhammad in appearance and they both were described by the Prophet as the 'Two princes of the youth in Paradise.'

Hasan was said to have many virtues, he was gentle, reserved and dignified. He was also very generous and liked to marry. Ibn Saa'd describes that he never heard a harsh or improper word from Hasan. While Hasan was sitting in Juma prayer, he would often have to listen to terrible things that Marwan, the governor of Medina, was saying about his father. Marwan then sent a very insulting message to Hasan. Instead of arguing and slandering him, he simply sent him a message "Go back and say to him from me, I will not try and erase something you said by insulting you back. My place of meeting and yours is before Allah, and if you have spoken the truth, then the Lord will reward you according to your truth, and if you have lied, then the Lord is terrible in vengeance."

THE KHALIFAH AND ABDICATION OF IMAM HASAN

After the death of Sayyidina 'Ali, Sayyidina Hasan was chosen as the next khalifa in 661 by the council in Kufa and supported by those back in the Hijaz (Makkah and Medina).

However, Mu'awiya in Syria did not recognise Hasan as the khalifah and led an army to Kufa to force him to abdicate and give up the title. In response, Hasan sent a small group of troops under 'UbaydAllah ibn al-Abbas to block Mu'awiya's advance until he could arrive with the main army. Meanwhile, Hasan was severely wounded by an assassination attempt by the Khwajirites, who had previously opposed Sayyidina 'Ali. This demoralised Hasan's troops and many of his army deserted. Mu'awiya meanwhile bribed 'UbaydAllah and most of the vanguard, who also defected.

Mu'awiya corresponded by letter with Hasan to convince him to abdicate. "You are asking me to settle the matter peacefully and surrender, but the situation concerning you and me today is like the one between your family and Abu Bakr after the death of the Prophet ﷺ... I have a longer period of reign [probably referring to his governorship], and I am more experienced, better in policies, and older in age than you ... If you enter into obedience to me now, you will accede to the khalifah after me."

So in August 661 (Rabi al-Thani 41 AH), Hasan signed a peace treaty with Mu'awiya on the basis that Mu'awiya should rule in compliance with the Qur'an and the Sunnah, a council appointed his successor, and that Hasan's supporters received amnesty.

Sayyidina Hasan abdicated the title in favour of Mu'awiya to avoid more war and bloodshed. Many Muslims criticised him as they felt Sayyidina Hasan was the rightful khalifah but he said, "I am no dishonourer of the Muslims, but I was loth to have you slaughtered for the sake of a kingdom." During the surrender ceremony, Mu'awiya asked Hasan to declare a public apology but instead, he told them he abdicated to avoid more bloodshed.

The Prophet ﷺ had predicted that Hasan would be the means for a peaceful resolution; "Truly this son of mine is a prince and perchance the Lord will unite through his means the two contending parties of the Muslims."

Mu'awiya then declared to the people: "God's protection is dissolved from anyone who does not come forth and pledge allegiance. Surely, I have sought revenge for the blood of 'Uthman, may God kill his murderers, and have returned the reign to those to whom it belongs despite the rancour of some people. We grant a respite of three nights. Whoever has not pledged allegiance by then will have no protection and no pardon. Everyone then rushed to take allegiance and Hasan left for Medina. Before he left Mu'awiya ordered him to quell the Khawjrite revolt near Kufa but Sayyidina Hasan refused, as he said he gave up fighting Mu'awiya for the sake of peace and community, not to begin fighting by his side. Hasan returned to Medina and spent the next nine years there.

THE PASSING OF IMAM HASAN

Hasan ibn 'Ali died on 2 April 670 (5 Rabi al-Thani 50 AH) from an illness or poisoning. Early sources are nearly unanimous that Hasan was poisoned, but there is some disagreement as to who it was. Possibly one of his wives, either Ja'da bint al-Ash'ath whereas other accounts accuses his Amirite wife Hind bint Suhayl. Or perhaps one of Hasan's servants gave a poisoned drink to the latter. In all cases, Mu'awiya is identified as the instigator. Mu'awiya reportedly convinced Hasan's wife to poison him with the promise of a large sum of money and marriage to his son, Yazid.

However, the early historian al-Tabari denied Mu'awiya's alleged role in Hasan's death, it's been suggested that this was out of concern for the faith of the common people. Some sources report that Yazid I (r. 680–683), proposed to Zaynab bint Ja'far ibn Abi Talib, who refused and instead preferred Hasan. The enraged Yazid subsequently had Hasan poisoned.

Hasan reportedly did not disclose the identity of his suspected poisoner to Husayn, fearing that the wrong person might be punished.

Husayn at the Bedside of the Dying Hasan, a folio from Fuzuli's Hadiqat al-Su'ada (Garden of the Blessed)

There were disagreements about where Sayyidina Hasan should be buried. He had wanted to be buried near his Grandfather, the Prophet Muhammad ﷺ, but Marwan opposed the idea so he was buried in the cemetery al-Baqi next to his mother.

This is an old photograph of the tomb in Al-Baqi Cemetery, which stood over the grave of Sayyidina Hasan and was sadly demolished in 1925 by the Wahabis in Saudi Arabia.

May Allah bless Sayyidina Hasan, ameen.

MU'AWIYA'S APPOINTMENT OF YAZID AS KHALIF

Ten years later, as Mu'awiya lay dying, he failed to honour the pact to allow the council at Medina to choose the next khalifah but instead chose his son, Yazid to be the next Umayyad khalif in 680 (61 A.H.).

Sayyidina Husayn refused to make the pledge of allegiance to Yazid because not only did it break the pact that had been made, it corrupted the principles of khalifah which is an elected position, rather than a kingship and was not the way of the Prophet ﷺ. In addition, the people of Syria and Iraq were already being oppressed by Yazid, who was ruthless in nature.

The people of Kufa began to send many letters, begging Husayn to come and free them from the tyranny of the Umayyads and particularly from the cruel rule of the Governor of Kufa, ibn Ziyad, who had already killed some of the Companions of the Prophet ﷺ. Not wanting to ignore their pleas and concerned about the conditions there, Sayyidina Husayn and 'UbaydAllah promised to come.

They set off from Makkah with Husayn's entire family including the women and children. He felt this was safer as the Umayyads could come to Medina and hold his family hostage, compromising his mission. His friends warned him against going, but he could not stand by while injustice was being done. He felt he had to do the right thing and act quickly. Husayn said: "I revolted not for wickedness nor for fame. Verily I rose only to seek for rectification in the nation of my grandfather, the Messenger of Allah ﷺ."

He sent a messenger to Kufa, informing the people that he was intending to come although they did not hear back. This messenger was killed by ibn Ziyad. Subsequent messengers were also killed by ibn Ziyad, but Husayn was not informed until he had almost arrived at Kufa. He was also told that the people had gone back on their word and that great danger lay ahead.

He informed his small army about the dangers of the situation, saying they were free to go with no guilt. Many left, but the Banu Hashim (the clan of Imam Husayn and the Prophet Muhammad ﷺ) stayed loyal by his side.

The Battle of Karbala

'Aisha narrated: The Prophet ﷺ said: "Gabriel informed me that my grandson al-Husayn will be killed after me in the land of al-Taff and brought me this *turbah* (mud/soil) and informed me that this is the soil of the place he will be martyred."

They rode across the desert towards Kufa and were eventually met by the Umayyad army of over 4000 men. Husayn and his men numbered only about 150. Yazid had ordered ibn Ziyad to get Sayyidina Husayn to give him his pledge, and if not, he must be killed. Yazid's generals met with Husayn who at first refused.

But as the days drew on, and Sayyidina Husayn's children were dying of thirst, he agreed to give the pledge. But Ibn Ziyad wanted him to be brought in chains in front of him (and probably have him executed anyway). Husayn said: "By Allah, I shall not give my oath to you like a humiliated one, and nor shall I flee like the captive." He would rather die fighting and all those around him agreed.

The battle began with all of Husayn's group fighting valiantly until all 72 of the men were killed. As they reached Sayyidina Husayn himself, some of the army including one of the commanders, were very reluctant to kill the Prophet's ﷺ grandson, but unbelievably, perhaps because they feared their own death at the hands of Ibn Ziyad, the army, who professed to be Muslims, carried out the orders. Even though the Messenger of Allah ﷺ said: *"Husayn is from me and I am from Husayn."*

The head of Husayn was then brought to Yazid who was initially very pleased but then regretted it when the people hated him for it. The Prophet ﷺ had predicted that Yazid would be the one who would be 'the first to subvert justice'. Husayn's family were brought to Yazid and were treated fairly and sent home a few days later. Thankfully, the women and some of the small children were not killed and their descendants continue to this day. May Allah bless the righteous people of the Prophet's ﷺ house - ameen.

After this tragic event, the Umayyad dynasty became established as the khulafah of the Muslims for the next four hundred years.

Hazrat Abu Shaikh narrates that in a gathering people were discussing how all those who were in any way involved in the killing of Imam Hussayn experienced the Wrath of Allah. An old man stood up and said, 'I too helped in his killing but look - nothing has happened to me.' Just then he stood up to attend to the lamp when he was caught up in flames and burned to his death. A similar incident is narrated by Imam Sa'ad in the Tareekh e Karbala.

May Allah bless Iman Husayn, ameen.

Illustration of the Battle of Karbala

Conclusion

In each of the Khulafah of Abu Bakr*, Umar*, Uthman* and Ali* we see some of the finest leaders the world has ever seen, who integrated justice, nobility and piety in their actions so that their lives serve to inspire future generations.

They had the momentous task of stabilising the Muslim Empire after the passing of the Prophet Muhammad ﷺ which could have so easily disintegrated into ruin, reverting to pre-Islamic days of tribal feuds and injustice. They each had trials to deal with such as the rebellions, false prophets and the might of the Byzantine and Persian Empires.

As the Prophet ﷺ predicted, however, after the death of Sayyidina Umar*, fighting between the Muslims grew more until the Rashidun Khalifah ended and the Ummayads took charge.

For many, their endings may seem terribly tragic, even though most achieved their wish to die as martyrs, but it is hard to believe that fellow Muslims would kill those who were so dear to the Prophet ﷺ. It is a reminder of the strength of the lower desires - that crave power and wealth, which can take over the heart of a believer.

Despite all the obstacles, their achievements were outstanding. During the Rashidun Kulafah, the Muslim Empire stretched as far southwest as Egypt, as far north as northern Syria, and to the East as far as the Sindh (present-day Pakistan). No other Empire spread so quickly and in such a peaceful way. The strict code of conduct in battle meant that innocent lives, animals and crops were protected.

The new religion had a positive impact on the society. Local people liked the new rules that Islam brought, (if they were governed correctly), either converting to Islam or practising their own faith. There were fair taxes and trade prospered.

In book three, we will look at the fascinating empires of the Ummayad, Abbasids and Ottomans as well as the Moghul and Islamic African empires, the best and the worst of the khulafah to come, the great scholars and mystics, as well as key events, in order to gain an understanding and overview of the rich and magnificent history of Islam, *inshaAllah*.

The Prophet ﷺ said: "The most compassionate of my Community towards my Community is Abu Bakr; the staunchest in Allah's Religion is 'Umar; the most truthful in his modesty is 'Uthman, and the best in judgement is 'Ali."

Tabarani narrated through Mu'adh that the Prophet ﷺ said, "I had a vision that I was put on one side of the Scale and my Nation was put on the other side, and I was heavier. Then Abu Bakr was put on one side and my Nation was put on one side, and Abu Bakr was heavier. Then 'Umar was put on one side and my Nation was put on the other, and 'Umar was heavier. Then 'Uthman was put on one side and my Nation on the other, and 'Uthman was heavier. Then the Scale was raised up."

The interior corridors at the Hassan II Mosque in Casablanca, Morocco.

ACKNOWLEDGEMENTS

It is impossible to fully honour and do justice to such luminous personalities such as the Rashidun Khulafah. May Allah forgive any mistakes and I pray this book serves to inform and inspire, by their excellent examples, all those who read it.

I would also like to thank Hana Horack-Elyafi, Ajsa Gutic and Rose McBride for editing and Sheikh Muhammad Hisham Kabbani for his constant guidance and teachings.

REFERENCES

Sahih al-Bukhari, published by Darussalam, Saudi Arabia, 1997

Men Around the Messenger by Khalid Muhammad Khalid, Al-Manara Press

History of the Caliphs by Jalalu'ddin A's Suyuti, Forgotten Books, 2018

The Islamic Conquest of Syria by al-Waqidi, Ta-Ha Publishers, 2005

Hadrat Abu Bakr Siddique by Prof. Masudul Hasan, Kitab Bhavan, 1997

The Rightly Guided Caliphs by Dr. Gibril Fouad Haddad 2023, ISCA, Fenton, USA

The Islamic History Podcast - https://islamichistorypodcast.com

Nahj al-Balagha: Sermon 75

Tareekh At-Tabari 2/449

Yaqeen Institute, The Firsts series, YouTube. Abu Bakr, 'Umar and 'Ali

https://www.youtube.com/@yaqeeninstituteofficial

https://quran.com/en/30:2/tafsirs/en-tafsir-maarif-ul-quran

https://sunnahmuakada.wordpress.com/2013/02/04/ali-ibn-abi-talib-his-merits

https://www.goodreads.com/author/quotes/20185188.Ali_ibn_Abi_Talib

http://lostislamichistory.com/jerusalem-and-umar-ibn-al-khattab/

http://legendaryleeph.blogspot.com/2016/03/the-life-of-khalid-ibn-walid-ra-sword.html

https://sunnah.com/

https://www.wikipedia.org

Images

Cover illustration by Hana Horack-Elyafi

Contents overleaf Geometric by Mokhtalif Art

Cover design and layout by Yasmin Watson

Page 40 Floral painting by Karen Winters

Adobe Stock Photos & Images

Shutterstock photos and Images

Other images from Wikicommons and the public domain

Traditionally in Islam, phrases of respect are added after mentioning Allah ﷻ, the Prophet Muhammad ﷺ, the other prophets, the Prophet's ﷺ Companions and the Saints.

ﷻ	*Jalla jalaluhu*: "May his Glory be glorified."
ﷺ	*Sallahu 'alayhi wa sallam*: "Peace and blessing be upon him.
عليهوسلم	*'Alayhi sallam*: "Peace be upon them."
رﮦ	*Radhiya llahu 'anhu*: "Well-pleased is Allah with them."
ق	*Qaddas-Allahu sirrah*: "May God sanctify their secret."

INDEX

Other Books by Halima Publishing!

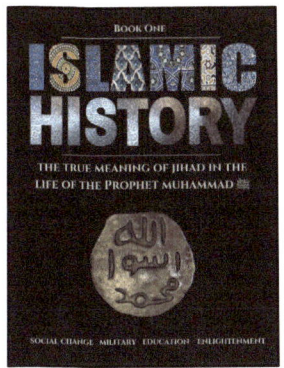

The first book in the series of Islamic History. We look at the life of the Holy Prophet Muhammad from the point of view of the four types of Jihad: Education and counsel, social change, military and self-defense and spirituality.Ideal for children aged 8+- adult.

ISBN 978 -1-9998027-2-1

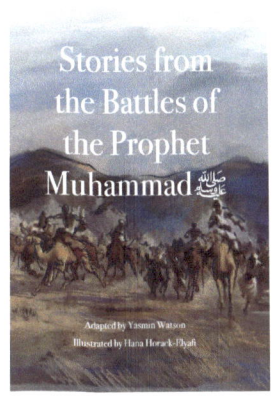

This exciting adaptation of the famous battles of early Islam follows the experiences of a fictional character, Abdul Karim, as he joins the Prophet Muhammad ﷺ in battle. Based on original sources. For children 8+

ISBN 979-8-8392260-8-1

In this book, children and young people can find out miraculous links with the Holy Qur'an and modern day science. With Montessori inspired science activities to do at home.

ISBN 978-1-9998027-0-7